I0820534

BROOM Magic

About the Authors

Chelsea Townsend is a lifelong Pagan, professional broom maker, and small business owner. She sells her brooms at several festivals and conferences each year as well as online, national wholesale orders, and by custom request. She believes in empowering others in their practice, and she loves to teach others how to make and use their tools. Visit her at BlossomsAndBrooms.com and on Facebook and Instagram.

Gypsey Teague (Callahan, FL) is an elder and high priestess in the Georgian tradition and high priestess in the Icelandic Norse tradition. She is also the author of *Steampunk Magic* (Weiser, 2013), *The Witch's Guide to Wands* (Weiser, 2015), and *Norse Divination* (Llewellyn, 2021).

BROOM Magic

How to Craft & Use Your Own Magical Besom

Chelsea Townsend
Gypsey Elaine Teague

LLEWELLYN
WOODBURY, MINNESOTA

First Edition
First Printing, 2025

Book design by Christine Ha
Cover design by Shira Atakpu
Interior illustrations
Broom photos (pages 192, 196, 202, 208, 216, and 222) by the Llewellyn Art Department
Images 1, 2, 4–11 by the Llewellyn Art Department, with direction from author
Images 3, 38 by the Llewellyn Art Department
Images 12–37, 39–77 provided by the author

Library of Congress Cataloging-in-Publication Data (Pending)
ISBN: 978-0-7387-7586-9

Llewellyn Publications
A Division of Llewellyn Worldwide Ltd.
2143 Wooddale Drive
Woodbury, MN 55125-2989
www.llewellyn.com

Printed in the United States of America

Other Books by Gypsey Elaine Teague

The Witch's Guide to Wands

Steampunk Magic

Norse Divination

Disclaimer

The contents of this book include the use of sharp tools and working with woods that could be dangerous if not handled properly. Please take precautions. The publisher and the author assume no liability for any injuries caused to the reader that may result from the reader's use of content contained in this publication and recommend common sense when contemplating the practices described in the work.

Contents

Foreword xv
Prologue xvii
Introduction 1

SECTION 1: Besom to Broom 3
Chapter 1: Broom History and Lore 5
Chapter 2: Understanding Your Broom 15
Chapter 3: The Essential Materials 21
Chapter 4: The Tools 31
Chapter 5: Basic Techniques 37
Chapter 6: Getting to Know Your Broom 47
Chapter 7: Brooms in Ritual and Magic 55

SECTION 2: Properties of Woods by Species 63
Alder 69
Apple 71
Ash 73
Beech 75
Birch 77
Black Locust 79
Black Walnut 81
Cedar, Deodar 83
Cedar, Eastern Red 85
Cherry 87
Chestnut 89
Cottonwood 91

Crepe Myrtle 93
Datura 95
Dogwood 97
Douglas Fir 99
Ebony 101
Elder 103
Elm 105
Fig 107
Gingko 109
Golden Rain Tree 111
Hackberry 113
Hawthorn 115
Hemlock 117
Hickory (Shagbark) 119
Holly 121
Hornbeam 123
Laurel 125
Magnolia 127
Maple 129
Mimosa 131
Mulberry 133
Oak 135
Olive 137
Orange 139
Osage Orange 141
Padauk (African Variety) 143
Peach 147
Pear 149
Pecan 151
Persimmon 153
Pine 155
Plum (Purple Leaf) 157
Poison Ivy 159
Poplar 163
Privet 165

Rosemary 167
Rowan 169
Spruce 171
Sumac 173
Supplejack 175
Sweetgum 177
Sycamore 179
Tulip Tree 181
Willow 183
Wisteria 185
Witch Hazel 187
Yew 189

SECTION 3: Broom Recipes 191
Cobwebber 193
Hearth Broom 197
Kitchen Broom with Knurl 203
Kitchen Broom with Hurl 209
Turkey Wing Whisk 217
Hawk Tail Whisk 223

Conclusion 229
Appendix A: Woods by Deities 231
Appendix B: Woods by Uses 237
Bibliography 241

Foreword

Witches and brooms—what a cliché. Well, I suppose it isn't really a cliché if it's true. As I'm sitting and writing this, in arm's reach is one of my hearth brooms, crafted by one of our late, great Ozark artisans. I don't have a literal hearth to clean, but this broom has been used to clean many a spiritual hearth. Each quarter when I refresh my altars, one of the last things I do is ritually sweep the space, then literally sweep it with my handy feedstore corn broom. When I get big news, one of the ways I cope with the processing of it is to stress (or sometimes rage) clean my house. There is little more satisfying to me than having a vigorous turn around my house sweeping out the dust while I sweep out the sadness, shock, anger, or confusion that news can sometimes bring.

Yes, as I'm sure many of my witch kin also do, I have a collection of brooms. Most of them have never touched the floor of my home but have done plenty of work! They guard the doorways, windows, or magical portals. They clear the space around my altars. They sweep away that bad energy just like my feedstore broom sweeps away the dust.

I have known and been friends with Gypsey for many years. I am in awe of the depth of knowledge she has about all the different woods that can be used in a broom. I met Chelsea at the same conference where Gypsey did and am happy that two of my collection were made by her. I love this collaboration because for an information sponge like me, learning more about broom history and getting deeper into the science aspect of the woods is my happy place.

As a scientist, I love the depth of wood species information presented within the pages of this book—so much so that it caused me to immediately inventory my collection of brooms to consider how to apply this new approach to my magical work. I had to stop and laugh out loud at the description of sweet gum, especially since I have to wrangle it constantly in my horse pasture.

As a hand crafter, I know there is magic in the making of any object. As a basket maker, I know a little about the skill needed to make a broom by hand. There is so much energy and magic woven into the intentional making of a handcrafted broom. This magic is available to tap into any time we use the broom. The delightful thing about this book is that it gave me new ideas about how to use them for magical work. I had never considered the depth to which I could use my brooms or the reverence the broom deserved before I read this book.

The hand crafter in me is chomping at the bit to try to make my own brooms as well. I love how accessible they make the methods and tools for crafting the different brooms in the book. True love of a craft is sharing knowledge for others to try their hand at it.

If you are like me, you never considered the idea of needing a book about brooms. I mean, they are just common household objects, right? I assure you I was totally wrong about that. This book opened up so many new avenues for my magical practice as well as my crafting. This is *the* book you need if you want to expand your magical horizons and add a powerful new ally in your practice. Now, if you will excuse me, I've got some sweeping to do!

—Debra Burris

Prologue

The old lady sat with her daughter and granddaughter in the small hut at the edge of the village. It had been a good year, and the larder was full as well as the pens with fat animals for slaughter. The small hut was getting a new roof next week courtesy of her nephew and her son-in-law in exchange for a pig and a goat, both of which would be slaughtered for the winter. And that was why the three women sat in the small hut talking and planning. In a week, the hut would be a mess of leaves and straw and thatch and muddy boot prints from those putting in the roof.

This was the first time her granddaughter would be present for the ritual, but it would not be the last. And, if the gods willed it, would not be the old lady's last either. But only they knew the future, and they didn't talk much to humans—even those who dealt on both sides of the veil.

Tonight was the first of three nights to make a new broom for the hut. She would make one for herself, her daughter would make one for her hut down the road, and her granddaughter would begin the long journey of learning how to make brooms. First would be the choosing of the broom straw. She made certain every piece was even and consistent. Tomorrow, she would make the shaft from a piece of straight and strong ironwood. It would be not only an instrument of cleaning but one of protection if the need arose.

Finally, on the third day, she would stitch it together and make certain it was ready to carry out its duties in the hut. After that, she would have a very private ritual behind closed windows and doors (lest those who did not approve of the old ways look in) and say goodbye to her old broom and welcome the new one. It was a tradition passed down from one generation to the next, and this time, it was her granddaughter who would learn the ways of the broom.

Introduction

Magic is all around us in the natural world. Witches are inspired by its beauty and power, often drawn to work with naturally derived implements to actualize this power. The authors of this book do not see this power as outside of the self but rather as a testament to our true nature. Connecting to the natural world is a part of daily ritual, ceremony, and practice.

This book is an essential resource for your practice; not only will you gain information on the history, lore, materials, and properties of brooms and broom making, but you will also receive guidance on how to personalize your broom in your own practice.

Your Guides

Chelsea came into broom making somewhat by accident after meeting her mentor, Broomsquire Dan Donaldson of Dewy Rose Brooms at an art festival. Fascinated by Dan's work, she became determined to learn the craft. For several months, Chelsea would drive hours each way to learn from Dan at his shop. Over the years, Chelsea has developed her own style and techniques not only of broom making but of brooms in mystical practice, many of which she will teach you in this book.

Chelsea met coauthor Gypsey at Mystic South in Atlanta. Gypsey is a Georgian Wiccan Elder and a Gyðia in the Icelandic Heathen Path. She is also a longtime artisan, woodworker, and maker of wands. With her extensive knowledge about the qualities of woods and their use in magical practice, Gypsey is a treasure trove of information about how brooms are affected by the wood used and how to most effectively put those materials to magical use.

Together, we are your perfect guides as you journey into the craft of broom making and its uses in the magical arts.

Getting Started

You will see that broom lore, like magical lore, has all kinds of contradictions and empty spaces. None of that matters; it is about what you feel and how you practice. Your intentions are woven into the very material your broom is made of, and that intention is what affects your practice. We encourage readers to really use this book, to write abundantly in the margins, and most of all, to make it, like your broom, completely your own.

Fly high!

SECTION 1: Besom to Broom

The first section of this book is designed to give you information on the history of brooms and how they fit into your magical life. We have worked to make everything as easy to relate to and use as possible, and it is our hope that you will find it as interesting to read and use as it was to make it.

Chapter 1
Broom History and Lore

The humble broom holds a rich and diverse history that spans cultures, continents, and centuries. From its early origins as a simple bundle of natural fibers to its modern adaptations in the era of technology, the broom has undergone a fascinating evolution that reflects changes in society, materials, and craftsmanship.

Early brooms can be traced back to ancient civilizations. In the ancient world, people used bundles of twigs, reeds, or other local, natural fibers to sweep away dirt and debris from their homes. These early brooms were primitive yet effective, utilizing readily available materials to maintain cleanliness.[1] The Brooklyn Museum has one in its collection that dates between 1539–1075 BCE.[2]

Different cultures around the world put their own unique spin on broom design and usage. For example, in Japan the *houki* broom was traditionally made from hemp palm fibers and was an essential tool in the practice of *Osoji*, the annual year-end cleaning ritual.[3] The religious practitioners of Jainism carry small brooms to sweep away ants and other tiny creatures as part

1. Anely M. Nedelcheva et al., "Plants Traditionally Used to Make Brooms in Several European Countries," *Journal of Ethnobiology and Ethnomedicine* 3, no. 20 (2007): https://doi.org/10.1186/1746-4269-3-20.
2. "Broom," Brooklyn Museum, accessed September 30, 2023, https://www.brooklynmuseum.org/opencollection/objects/118434.
3. "Shuro Houki: Hemp-Palm Broom," trans. Tae Yamaguchi, reviewed Marina Izumi, Japanese Traditional Crafts, Japanese Traditional Culture Promotion & Development Organization, accessed September 30, 2023, https://www.jtco.or.jp/en/japanese-crafts/?act=detail&id=300&p=30&c=29.

of their belief of nonviolence.[4] In this book, we'll be discussing brooms of the Western and European tradition, which modern witches often call a *besom*.

The Besom

The besom started as nothing more than a bundle of sticks, twigs, or grasses tightly wound around a stick. The word *besom* has its origins in Old English and is derived from the word *besma*, which referred to a bundle of twigs or a broom. Over time, this term evolved into the Middle English *beseme* with the same meaning.[5] These besoms were typically made in the home and, due to their rather fragile nature, required repair regularly.

Broomcorn

For natural brooms today, we use a plant in the sorghum family with the conveniently descriptive name *broomcorn* (*Sorghum bicolor*). The true origin of the plant is unknown, but the current theory is that it originated in Sudan and Saharan Africa with the other sorghums.[6] Sometime around the 1600s, the plant made its way to Italy and then the rest of Europe and finally the colonies.[7]

The broomcorn plant looks much like standard corn even though it is of a completely unrelated species. This upright grass can grow anywhere from 6 to 15 feet tall. Unlike corn, it does not produce a cob. Instead, the top tassel becomes the brush of the broom after being dried and de-seeded.[8] It is easily grown throughout the United States, but planting, harvesting, and

....

4. Ron Cherry and Hardev Sandhu, "Insects in the Religions of India," *American Entomologist* 59, no. 4 (2013): 200–202, https://www.researchgate.net/figure/Jain-monks-wear-mesh-over-their-faces-to-avoid-inhaling-insects-and-carry-soft-brooms-to_fig1_262855310.
5. "Besom," Merriam-Webster, accessed September 5, 2024, https://www.merriam-webster.com/dictionary/besom.
6. Galaihalage K. S. Ananda et al., "Wild Sorghum as a Promising Resource for Crop Improvement," *Frontiers in Plant Science* 11 (2020), https://doi.org/10.3389/fpls.2020.01108; Janoš Berenji et al., "Origin, History, Morphology, Production, Improvement, and Utilization of Broomcorn [Sorghum bicolor (L.) Moench] in Serbia," *Economic Botany* 65, (2011): 190–208, https://doi.org/10.1007/s12231-011-9155-2.
7. P. R. Carter et al., "Broomcorn," Alternative Field Crops Manual, accessed September 30, 2023, https://hort.purdue.edu/newcrop/afcm/broomcorn.html.
8. Carter et al., "Broomcorn."

processing is all done by hand and is thus very labor intensive and therefore expensive. Most of the broomcorn that crafters use today comes from Mexico due to cheaper labor and land. Other sources of broomcorn include China, Paraguay, Hungary, and Indonesia.[9] Many modern broom makers, Chelsea included, grow at least some of their broomcorn themselves.

Most sources state that Benjamin Franklin brought broomcorn to the United States in the early eighteenth century. In one story, Franklin saw a woman in Philadelphia with an imported whisk on which he found a single seed that he later planted and propagated as a novelty crop.[10] Another story says that a friend gifted him a whisk from France to dust his beaver hat, and Franklin found a single seed on it.[11] There are yet more stories about Franklin, but unfortunately none can be confirmed. We do have a record of him having written a letter to his sister in which he sent some seeds from Virginia and asked her to plant them.[12] After the plant's introduction, broomcorn quickly became an important crop throughout New England and the colonies.

The eighteenth and nineteenth centuries brought about significant changes in manufacturing and materials. This period witnessed the transition from individually handcrafted brooms to mass-produced ones, thanks to advancements in mechanization. In Hadley, Massachusetts, in the late 1700s, Levi Dickinson was farming broomcorn to sell as animal feed, and he is credited with crafting the tools and techniques that turned homemade, handmade broomcorn besoms into sturdier, longer-lasting brooms salable on a commercial scale. Dickinson then manufactured and sold them to everyone in neighboring communities, sparking a new industry in New England."[13]

. . . .

9. Karen Hobbs, *Swept Away: The Vanishing Art of Broom Making* (Schiffer Publishing, 2017), 5.
10. Editors of the *American Agriculturist*, *Broom-Corn and Brooms: A Treatise on Raising Broom-Corn* and *Making Brooms on a Small or Large Scale*, new and revised ed. (Orange Judd Company, 1908), 10–11.
11. National Garden Association, "Harvesting Broom Corn—Knowledgebase Question," accessed October 1, 2023, https://garden.org/frogs/view/14292/.
12. "From Benjamin Franklin to Jane Mecom, 21 February 1757," Founders Online, National Archives, accessed September 30, 2023, http://founders.archives.gov/documents/Franklin/01-07-02-0048.
13. J. Bryan Lowder, "How the Broom Became Flat," Slate, June 6, 2012, https://slate.com/human-interest/2012/06/broom-history-how-it-became-flat.html.

Broom Evolution

The broom went through a major evolution once more in the early 1800s by the Shaker community in Watervliet, New York. Here, Theodore Bates made the first broom vise, which is used to make flat brooms, as are common today instead of the round brooms that were being used previously. By pressing and holding the bristles flat, one could sew heavy twine throughout, forcing the broom to hold that shape permanently.[14]

Broomcorn production boomed in the United States until the 1950s, when plastic bristles became popular and vacuum ownership increased.[15] With the advent of the North American Free Trade Agreement (NAFTA) in 1994, Mexican brooms were permitted into the United States duty free, so Mexico was now able to supply American consumers with cheap brooms that small, American broom factories could not compete with. The American broom industry was dead.

In recent years, there has been a dramatic increase in public interest in folk arts. While commercial American broomcorn brooms may be a thing of the past, the art of broom making is seeing a resurgence, and corn brooms are not only becoming more available, but more beautiful as well. According to the Observatory of Economic Complexity, sales of corn broom increased by over $10 million between 2020 and 2021.[16]

Folklore and Traditions

The magical properties of brooms vary depending on cultural beliefs, traditions, and individual interpretations. In many traditions, sweeping with a broom is not just about cleaning physical dirt but also about clearing away negative energy and warding off evil spirits.[17] Whether used for flying

14. "Shaker Made: Agriculture & Industry," The Shakers: Americas Quiet Revolutionaries, New York State Museum, accessed February 13, 2025, https://exhibitions.nysm.nysed.gov/shakers/industry.html.
15. Kate Morgan, "The Sweeping Appeal of Handcrafted Brooms," *Washington Post*, November 3, 2023, https://www.washingtonpost.com/home/2023/11/03/craft-brooms-enjoy-increased-popularity/.
16. "Brooms/Brushes of Vegetable Material," The Observatory of Economic Complexity, accessed February 6, 2024, https://oec.world/en/profile/hs/broomsbrushes-of-vegetable-material?redirect=true.
17. Patti Wigington, "Make Your Own Besom," Learn Religions, updated September 26, 2018, https://www.learnreligions.com/make-your-own-besom-2562738.

through the night sky or for sweeping away negative energy, brooms hold a special place in magical symbolism and practice.

Ceremonies and Rituals

In many African and Indigenous American cultures, ceremonial sweeping is used to cleanse a space of evil influences and create a positive, harmonious environment. For example, the Adangme culture in Africa ritually cleanses their towns by sweeping all of the roads and compounds.[18]

In Chinese folklore, sweeping just before the Lunar New Year symbolizes sweeping away of misfortune to make way for good luck and prosperity. However, sweeping on the day of the Lunar New Year sweeps away good fortune. One European rhyme says that a broom purchased in May is unlucky: "Buy a broom in May / sweep a friend away."[19]

After the release of Alex Haley's 1976 novel about slavery, *Roots: The Saga of an American Family*, and its miniseries adaptation, jumping the broom at the end of a wedding became a common practice in many Black and African American weddings as a way to connect with one's history and has become one of the most well-known broom traditions of our age.[20]

The origin of this tradition is rather complex, and there is debate as to whether it started in West Africa, where the broom was used to protect against evil spirits by waving it over the couple to be married, or in the European Roma community as a way to celebrate marriage when they were not otherwise allowed to do so.[21] Jumping the broom is also used in modern Pagan weddings as a callback to the tradition's European origins, with the

....

18. Hugo Huber, "Adangme Purification and Pacification Rituals (West Africa)," *Anthropos* 53, no. 1/2 (1958): 161–91, http://www.jstor.org/stable/40453193.
19. Nicola Minney, "Superstitious in the Countryside: Ten British Farming Superstitions," *The MERL* (blog), October 31, 2020, https://merl.reading.ac.uk/blog/2020/10/superstitious-countryside/.
20. Tyler Parry, "Jumping the Broom and the American Cultural Divide," Black Perspectives, African American Intellectual History Society, February 7, 2018, https://www.aaihs.org/jumping-the-broom-and-the-american-cultural-divide/.
21. Christopher R. Fee and Jeffrey B. Webb, eds., "Jumping the Broom," in *American Myths, Legends and Tall Tales: An Encyclopedia of American Folklore*, vol. 2: G–P (ABC-CLIO, 2016), 546; Ceija Stojka, *The Memoirs of Ceija Stojka, Child Survivor of the Romani Holocaust*, trans. Lorely E. French (Camden House, 2022), 10-11.

stick of the broom representing the male energy and the brush representing the female.

There are many ways a couple can jump the broom, but in general, a broom that is highly decorated in ribbons and flowers is laid on the floor in front of the couple, and together they jump over it to represent sweeping away their previous lives to enter into domestic life.[22] We will talk more about the wedding ceremony and "jumping the broom" in chapter 7.

The Boo Hag

The Boo Hag is a mythical creature often found in Gullah folklore and the broader cultural traditions of the South Carolina Lowcountry in the United States. Rooted in African American folklore and influenced by African, European, and Native American beliefs, the Boo Hag myth is captivating.

According to the legends, Boo Hags are skinless, shapeshifting beings that do not exist physically in the world. The spirit of the Boo Hag slips into the victim's home through small openings such as keyholes, cracks, or gaps around doors and windows and takes over the sleeping victim, who might wake feeling exhausted, drained, and even sickly, all due to the Boo Hag's visit.

To protect themselves from the Boo Hag, the Gullah people devised a variety of countermeasures. One common method was to place a straw broom near the entrance of the home. The Boo Hag, who is compulsively driven to count objects, becomes fixated on counting the bristles of the broom. This counting obsession prevents the Boo Hag from entering the home and tormenting the sleeping occupants before the sun rises and the potential victim awakens.[23]

22. Alan Dundes, "'Jumping the Broom': On the Origin and Meaning of an African American Wedding Custom," *The Journal of American Folklore* 109, no. 433 (1996): 324–29, https://doi.org/10.2307/541535.
23. Shari Tingle, "Boo Hags Going Bump in the Night," CHStoday, 6AM City Inc., October 26, 2020, https://chstoday.6amcity.com/boo-hags-going-bump-in-the-night.

The Witch's Broomstick

The association between witches and broomsticks is an enduring part of witchcraft folklore and imagery, and there are several theories for why witches are so often depicted as riding broomsticks.

In medieval Europe, it was believed that witches would use a special salve containing hallucinogenic substances including aconite and belladonna.[24] Witches would apply this ointment to various parts of their bodies, including their genitals, which would create hallucinations of flying or floating. Brooms were believed to be a convenient way to apply the ointment, and this association led to the idea of witches flying on broomsticks.

A common spring ritual in Europe was for the village women to jump and dance while straddling their brooms to encourage their crops to grow tall. It is easy to see how this type of sympathetic magic could be interpreted as flying on the brooms.[25]

Another theory suggests that the broomstick, with its long, slender shape, came to symbolize a phallic object, and the act of witches riding brooms may have been seen as a form of sexual symbolism or taboo-breaking in a conservative society.[26] Brooms were also associated with domesticity and female work, as are other icons of witchcraft including cauldrons, jars of herbs, the knife, the chalice, and candles. The idea of witches using broomsticks and other household tools to assert power subverted traditional gender roles and reinforced stereotypes about witches being dangerous and subversive women.[27]

During the European witch hunts of the late medieval and early modern periods, women and men accused of witchcraft were often subjected to torture and pressured to confess to supernatural acts, including flying on broomsticks. These confessions were obtained under duress, and the association between witches and broomsticks became further ingrained in the

24. Clive Harper, "The Witches' Flying-Ointment," *Folklore* 88, no. 1 (1977): 105–106, https://doi.org/10.1080/0015587X.1977.9716057.
25. Sarah Pruitt, "Why Do Witches Ride Brooms? The History Behind the Legend," History, updated August 9, 2023, https://www.history.com/news/why-witches-fly-on-brooms; Robin Skelton, *The Practice of Witchcraft* (Porcépic Books, 1990), 46–47.
26. Dylan Thuras, "Sex, Drugs, and Broomsticks: The Origins of the Iconic Witch," Atlas Obscura, October 23, 2014, http://www.atlasobscura.com/articles/why-do-witches-ride-brooms.
27. Thuras, "Sex, Drugs, and Broomsticks."

collective imagination. After being arrested in 1493, a priest named Guillaume Edelin became the first to claim that he'd ridden on a broom. Notably, he'd also been publicly critical about the church's concern over witches. In fact, the earliest depiction we have of a witch on a broom was only two years earlier in a book titled *Le Champion des Dames (The Defender of Ladies)* by French poet Martin Le Franc.[28] Over time, these ideas about witches riding broomsticks became popularized in folklore and storytelling, cementing the image of the witch on a broomstick in popular culture.

Wards, Divination, and Other Uses

This taste of broom history and folklore should give you a sense of the importance of the humble broom. From the practical to the paranormal, there is no doubt that brooms are part of our everyday consciousness more than we might even realize. Here are a few more magical uses that have survived through folk traditions:

- In Appalachian folk traditions, if a broom fell while someone was standing nearby, it was thought to be an omen or sign about future events.
- In China, occupation of a spirit was indicated if a broom that is suspended starts to rotate or swing.
- Placing a broom outside your door, particularly with the bristles facing upward, was thought to provide protection against evil spirits and negative energy. However, it is more likely this is a proactive practice to keep the bristles from becoming soiled by floor dust or chewed on by small animals.
- Some practitioners use a broom to sweep a protective barrier or ward around a space, helping to keep unwanted energies or entities at bay. This practice is still observed in some cultures today.

The next time you reach for the sweeper, invite yourself to take a moment to acknowledge that, truly, the art of broom making and usage is a part of our collective human lineage.

....

28. Pruitt, "Why Do Witches Ride Brooms?"

Broom Etiquette

Sandy, one of Gypsey's friends, is a witch focused on folk magic. She is the child of people transplanted from Appalachia to Miami, Florida. Her experience living in both areas has given her a unique and complex understanding of broom magic and when not to apply it. We asked her to share that heritage. Sandy wrote the following:

> *Broom stuff,* as I call it, was one of the few culturally embedded folk magic realms that survived in my family when my parents came "down from the mountain," as they say in West Virginia, and moved to Miami, Florida, in 1962, leaving behind what they viewed as their limited upbringings.
>
> Elder West Virginians had the same rules but said they were for good luck, keep'n the devil out, or to "keep theirs and ours apart." Modern Miami folks said this was for hygiene or *logical systems* (regularly scheduled cleaning). However, there are other times that require such thorough cleansing. Here are a few of the rules:
>
> > *Rule 1:* New home, new broom. Never bring a broom when you move. Break or burn the old one. A used broom in your new place goes outside for garbage pickup. Likewise, new broom for new situations: wedding, divorce, house remodel, after a break-in, etc. Discard the old one before you bring in the new one.
> >
> > *Rule 2:* Never use your broom at someone else's house or anywhere in a public area like a street. Your landscaping broom never comes inside. Sweep inside clockwise from east to west. Sweep to clean and for good order.
> >
> > *Rule 3:* Sweep after an argument, after an illness or mishap, and after a period of tight finances. Play your favorite music while doing this, moving clockwise through the house in a clearly ceremonial way.
> >
> > *Rule 4:* Only *qualified* sweepers allowed. Girls were told to help "start sweeping" with their "own broom" when they

seemed "grown enough." Men and boys did landscape or storm sweep ups outside.

Rule 5: Your house, your broom. Drama happened when family pecking orders were challenged by people grabbing brooms. This manifested negativity in the house. If you had a cleaning service, they used the vacuum.

I uphold the broom rules to clean emotional and spiritual spaces while upkeeping physical ones. I sweep once a week as a meditation. I have cast away brooms when romances, phases of life, and jobs have ended. I have, upon request, swept in others' homes, such as after a death or when pecking orders changed, but never out of spite. I'm startled when people ask me to "violate" broom rules. I find ways to "lose" brooms while helping others move or offer to do dishes instead of sweep after parties.

I am saddened that some people set aside rich and important ties to their family histories and places of origin. Past people were more observant and situationally aware than they are given credit for. There are scientific reasons for broom rules, but ancestors had instinctual understandings of the need for positive metaphysical action.

Chapter 2
Understanding Your Broom

Brooms are simple tools, but knowing their makeup is important. After all, when using a broom in practice, one must know the top from the bottom. And when making brooms, one must know what parts we are working on in order to understand instructions or ask (or answer) questions from other broom makers.

There are many styles of brooms, including the kitchen broom, hearth broom, and cobwebber, as well as styles of whisks, which are a part of the broom family, including the turkey wing and the hawk tail, all of which have instructions included later in this book. These brooms are all generally accepted types, though they may be styled differently by each broom maker. Individual broom makers have created other types as well and variations on those types. Broom makers like Chelsea prefer not to define most of their brooms and allow the stick to determine how the final broom will be shaped and used.

Anatomy of Broomcorn

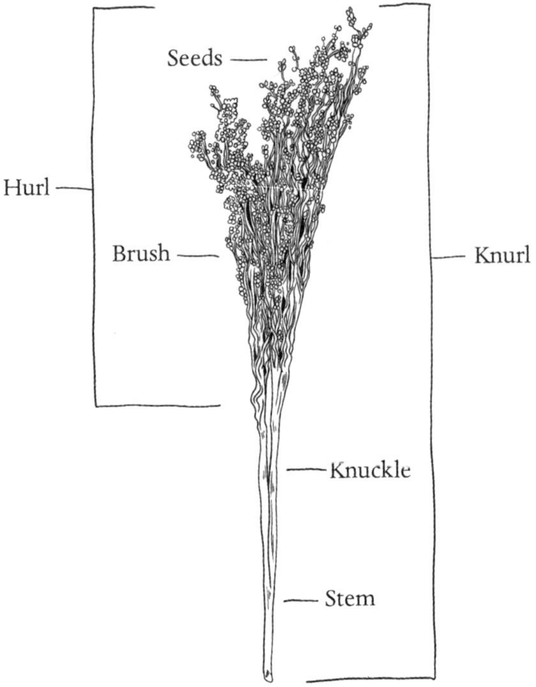

Image #1: Anatomy of broomcorn

First, we need to discuss the anatomy of the plant that we make brooms from, broomcorn. Here are the essential parts:

- *Nurl or Knurl:* The entire top portion of the plant, including the top of the stalk all the way to the seeds at the tip.
- *Brush:* The bristles on the end of a broom.
- *Hurl:* Only the fluffy part of the broomcorn, disconnected from the stem, to be used in broom making.
- *Seeds:* Seeds are produced at the tips of the hurl, at the very top of the plant. They are removed for broom making unless left on for decoration.
- *Knuckle:* Where the brush meets the stem.
- *Stem:* The solid top of the plant before it becomes brush.
- *Stalk:* The entire broomcorn plant.

Anatomy of a Broom

Next, you need to learn the anatomy of the broom itself. Here are those essential parts:

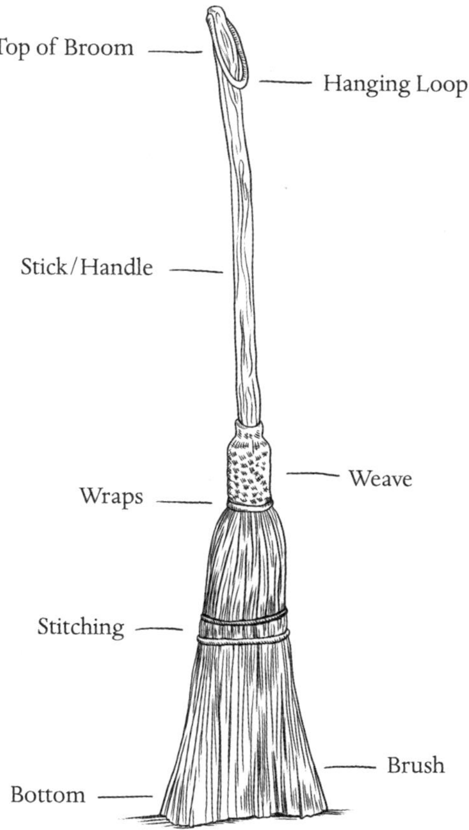

Image #2: Anatomy of a broom

- *Top:* The end of the handle farthest from the brush, where there is usually a hanging loop.
- *Stick:* The part of the broom that you hold. The stick can be made of many materials, including wood branches, deer antlers, wrought iron, and more.
- *Wraps:* The twine that encircles the broomcorn, holding it securely to the stick. Sometimes the wraps can be seen and are

decorative as well as utilitarian, and sometimes they are covered with reed or broomcorn stems.

- *Weave:* The decorative section at the top of the broomcorn that finishes the broom and ensures it will not fall apart in use. There are many ways to weave, but the most common is a simple over-under pattern that results in a basket weave design. The weave can be made from the stems of the broomcorn that make up your broom or from basket reed, cornstalks, or other materials that are added on top of the wraps.
- *Brush:* The business end of the broom, where the broomcorn touches the floor when sweeping. The brush can be left a natural straw color or dyed. If making an ornamental or ritual broom, many things can be used as the brush, including grass, twigs, dried flowers, and more.
- *Stitching:* Twine that has been wrapped around the brush of the broom, creating either a round or flat shape. It controls the brush and keeps it tight, making a more efficient sweeper.
- *Bottom:* The tips of the broomcorn.

Magical Anatomy

A witch's tool kit is not just confined to a wand and an athame. We have a myriad of tools at our disposal, and the broom is a multifunctional one. In theory as well as practice, a broom is more than just a cleaning tool. A broom is a linear, vascular, once-living thing with attributes and properties unique to the individual species of the wood. And with that energy, similar to a wand, each wood radiates at a different frequency, if we may use that metaphor. Drawing a parallel to the wand, a broom may also be used as and considered a casting tool.

Therefore, let's look at the broom as both a cleaning and casting tool and move on from there. Remember, do not confuse cleaning with cleansing. A broom cleans. It sweeps. It dusts. It does not cleanse.

First, think of a broom as a large wand. There is a positive and negative to the broom just as there is a positive and negative to a wand. Not positive and negative as in right or wrong or good or bad, but more like a battery. Neither end of a battery is right or wrong; they are instead conduits of energy, and, like a battery, you must have both ends working to draw energy from it.

Now, continuing the wand metaphor, you may cast as easily with a broom as a wand, albeit a very large wand, but a wand nonetheless. Think of the bristle end of your broom as the negative end and the shaft end as the positive. When you cast with a wand, you cast, most of the time, with the pointy end. There isn't a better way to describe the positive end of the wand. You don't have to literally point the handle end at the quarters or out into the aether; you only have to tip the broom in that direction.

Still working on the analogy of a battery, you do not want to ever seal the positive end of the broom. Leave a small section in the middle of the handle end and seal everything else. It is the same as sealing over the positive end of a battery and expecting it to conduct electricity. If you are treating the broom as a large wand, then you are directing the energy of the wood, powered by the energy of the user, outward to whatever target there is—and there is always a target. For without a target, the energy would go forever outward, and that would be a less than good thing.

The odds of a successful action are improved when the energy of the broom matches the task. An example of this would be trying to perform a healing circle with a poison ivy wand. Nothing you do is going to make the poison ivy wand perform anything positive. It's just not in the magical makeup of the wood.

A non-magical example would be right-handed scissors to a right-handed individual. The scissors function perfectly and cut cleanly and evenly. A left-handed user, though, would have a less-than-perfect outcome using right-handed scissors in their left hand. But with left-handed scissors, their outcome would be equally successful to their right-handed counterpart. In the following chapters, you will learn the properties of each wood and how to find the best broom type for whatever ritual or use you need it for.

Broom Consciousness

We will mention often throughout this book that brooms "know." They are not sentient as humans are, but they are cognizant of their surroundings and their place in the universe, as all other living things are.

Those of you who doubt that a broom or a wand or an athame has a consciousness have never actually gotten to know your tools. We have heard friends say that the fairies have taken their athame and hidden it or moved their wand from where it was left. The Fae may have had a hand in some things, but at times, the tools themselves "go" other places if you are not paying attention to them or are mistreating them.

You have paid a great deal for your tools, not necessarily in money but maybe in time and energy. Hopefully your tools were made by you or by another witch that you knew since not everyone forges athames and bolines. This creation binds you and your tools together. However, if you were gifted or purchased a tool from someone you didn't know or didn't know well, then you may still be bound to the tool through use, care, and respect. That's how you get the best results in circle or during rituals.

Chapter 3
The Essential Materials

Unlike the tools used in broom making (discussed in the next chapter), most of the materials for broom making are a little more difficult to obtain since they're not commonly found in stores, but they can be found online. There is room for experimentation, but we suggest starting with the following due to relative availability and cost.

Basic Materials

Here is a list of all the materials we use in our own broom crafting.

Nylon Twine

We use #18 nylon twine to do our wrapping and weaving, but you may go up to #24, which is thicker if you prefer a chunkier look or if that is all that is available. Nylon twine is very strong and consistent and comes in many colors. Cotton and linen twines, on the other hand, are relatively weak, and we have even broken hemp twine while weaving.

7- or 9-Ply Waxed Linen Thread

Waxed linen thread is strong, not slick, and comes in many colors. There are other threads and lines that can be used, but we appreciate the color selection of linen thread and the wax provides great traction when stitching. Feel free to experiment on your own, just remember that it must be quite strong to withstand years of use.

¼-Inch Flat or Flat-Oval Basket Reed

Basket reed is commonly used as an overlay to the wraps, making a decorative weave. The reed is easily dyed with common grocery store dye and can make a simple broom look a bit more interesting. Weaving with basket reed (or other materials such as leather, cut broomcorn stalks, fabric, etc.) allows you to introduce other colors, textures, and intentions into your broom as well as strengthening the broomcorn's attachment to the handle.

22-Inch Broomcorn Hurl

Hurl is just the loose, brush end of the broomcorn removed from the stalk and de-seeded. It makes up the business end of the broom. You can purchase hurl in several lengths shorter than 22 inches, but we prefer to keep it simple and just go for the longest. That way we can make any size broom or whisk just by trimming it to the correct length without having to purchase and store multiple sizes of hurl. Longer trimmings can also be used to make smaller whisks and brushes.

Craft Broomcorn

This is the upper stem of broomcorn with hurl still attached to the stem and de-seeded. There are other types of broomcorn available, such as duck blind broomcorn, but craft broomcorn is a higher-quality product and what we use to make brooms.

Preparation of Your Materials

Since the broom is a very personal magical instrument, your intention when making your broom will energetically, and possibly visibly, reflect in your work. Remember that you are working with natural materials that will easily absorb the energy you radiate. And as we previously discussed, the materials themselves will also have an energy of their own that must be considered in your process.

Approach your broom making with a clear head and open mind. Feel free to open a circle around your workspace and invoke the god or goddess that matches your intention, if that is your tradition. When ready, settle into your workspace and breathe deeply. Stretch your shoulders and back. Play some music or enjoy the silence.

Let's get started.

Prepare Your Stick

In our workshop, everything we do is intentional, and it begins with selecting the stick. Remember, the stick is another name for the broom's handle. The type of wood you want to use, where and how you find it, what condition it was in, the surrounding woods—all of it affects the energy of the stick. The first stick you pick up may not be the stick you will want to use. Find the one that feels like it's already yours.

If you decide to cut a living stick from a tree, be sure to ask permission from the tree and landowner first, and thank them before you leave. If you find your stick on the ground, be sure to thank the environment around it. And remember that almost anything can be used as a handle, including replacement handles that you can buy at the hardware store. Heck, even something like a flute can be used as a handle! Use what speaks to you.

Choose a stick that is between ¾ inch and 1 inch in diameter and a length that is comfortable for you to hold and for the type of broom you intend to make. We use a stick approximately 46 inches long for a kitchen broom, 18 inches for a hearth broom, and varying lengths for a cobwebber. All of these lengths are just suggestions based on our physical comfort and convenience. However, often the stick will tell you what length it wants to be either by shape or feel. Don't be afraid to use sticks that are wonky with zigzags or curves if that appeals to you, though it may make building the broom a bit more difficult.

Image #3: Broom types

Once you have selected your stick, it must be dried at least six months so that it won't shrink once the broom is tied on. It is best to dry a broomstick somewhere with excellent air circulation and out of direct sunlight and weather. A dry basement is an ideal location since it is usually cool and protected from the sun, but just getting propped up in the corner of your house is fine.

Bark or No Bark?

After drying, some species such as pine have very loose bark, and on others like oak, the bark sticks tight. Drying conditions can affect this as well. You can test for this by trying to chip off the bark where you cut it. If the bark flakes off, it must be removed so that it doesn't flake while it is being used.

Different woods have different characteristics in their appearance after the bark is removed. We love the deep, dark inner wood of sweetgum with the bark removed, for example. And the bark of ash has a wonderful texture and remains tight, but it also has a wonderful wood under that bark that may be exposed by removing it. It all just depends on the stick and your preferences.

In our opinion, bark removal is one of the hardest parts about broom making, but there are a few ways to make it easier. If you have access to a power washer, start there. Power washers shoot water so fast that it can take off skin, so please be careful and wear long pants and boots to protect your legs, feet, and toes! We lay the stick on the ground and hold it in place with a booted foot. Spray the stick with the wand of the power washer about an inch away from it. Sometimes it takes a minute or two for the bark to loosen. After power washing, set the stick somewhere out of direct sunlight to dry overnight.

If you don't have a power washer, or if the bark still does not come off after using one, you can put the stick into a vise and use a spoon carving knife, a spokeshave, or a drawknife to cut the bark off. To prevent marring the stick in the vise, you can wrap the part of the stick that will be in the vise in leather or another soft, thick material. Be sure to learn how to use any of these tools properly, as they are very, very sharp and can seriously hurt you if used incorrectly. We have found that there are times when each of these tools comes in handy; it just depends on your stick and your intentions for it.

Finishing Your Stick

If you removed the bark, sand the stick well so that it is comfortable to hold. Start with 180-grit sandpaper followed by 220 grit. You can sand by hand, but a palm sander makes faster work of it. Check for any imperfections in the wood that you may not want to include in your broom or may weaken it. It's easier to stop at this point and start over than to finish the project and then discover that you missed a small blemish or rotted area that will cause your broom to fail when you need it.

After sanding, use a knife or band saw to cut the bottom of the stick to a gradual point about 2 inches long, like a pencil tip. This point prevents an empty void at the bottom of the stick inside the brush once everything is pulled together by stitching.

Image #4: Pointed end of stick

Drill a ⅛-inch hole through the stick about 3 inches from the tip of the pointed end, which is where the twine will be tied for wrapping the broomcorn, securing it to the stick. Use your sandpaper to lightly smooth the hole to prevent any catches on the twine. Drill a ¼-inch hole about 1½ inches from the top of the stick, where you will thread a loop for hanging the broom.

Image #5: Hanging hole

After sanding and drilling, it is time to put a finish on your stick to protect it from dirt and skin oils. Finishes vary depending on the look and feel you want for your stick. We prefer a very natural feel, so we use Danish Oil, which can be purchased at any major hardware store or online. If we're looking for a little shine, satin polyurethane works very well. There are many other options such as varnish, wax, tung oil, and more that can all be used to finish the stick. Each type of finish has characteristics that you may or may not want, such as changing the color of the bark or wood as well as the finish's brittleness or flexibility. It is also possible to paint or stain your stick if you want a specific color or effect, or even carve in runes or spells. You'll want to experiment and see what you like; the options are endless.

Prepare the Broomcorn

Broomcorn is not available in stores, but it is easily ordered online. There are two types of broomcorn that you can order for making brooms: craft and hurl. Craft is broomcorn that has only had its seeds removed and is otherwise unprocessed. Hurl is processed broomcorn in which the seeds and stem have been removed, leaving only the loose brush of the broomcorn. Either is acceptable; however, there are tricks to using both that make your process easier and more enjoyable and will give different effects to the look of your final broom. The broom recipes in this book will introduce you to several of these effects.

Sorting Craft Broomcorn

If you chose to order craft broomcorn, the material will need to be sorted into selected lengths and quality. We do this in two steps: first, by making two piles as we sort, one for inner stems which are those that are broken or otherwise imperfect, and one for outer stems, which are those that are of the best quality to be seen and used, and secondly by length.

Some types of brooms have layers, where the outside layer leaves the stem exposed, so when you receive your shipment, each stem needs to be sorted into inner and outer quality. The imperfect stems are perfect for the inner layers because their faults will not be seen. Some of the faults you will find include broken or cracked stems, weak brush that is floppy and limp, insides that are clustered into a secondary, inner stem, or hard, shrunken stem tips.

You can test for broken stems by gently trying to bend them and rotating them as you visually inspect them. If the stem breaks in half or shows a crack or split, it should be used as an inner. Sometimes the inside of the brush doesn't separate well from the stem when it is growing, and you will have a cluster of undifferentiated brush, and it will be best used as an inner. Sometimes the bottom tip of the stem will be shrunken and hard. These are difficult to weave, so we use them as inners.

The outer stems, on the other hand, should be even in circumference, have no breaks or cracks, and have strong brush that is not floppy. These are the stems that are the most able to withstand being woven and will be seen once the broom is complete.

After sorting into inner and outer stems, we sort the craft broomcorn into different lengths. This way, when you make brooms that you do not want to trim but leave wispy on the end, you know that the broomcorn will all be similar lengths to make a relatively even bottom.

Each broom maker has their own method to do this, but this is how we do it in our shop. First, label eight 5-gallon buckets with masking tape: four for inner stalks and four for outer stalks. The inner and outer buckets are then sorted by size: longer than 34 inches, between 28 inches and 34 inches, between 22 inches and 28 inches, and shorter than 22 inches. You may use different measurements if you like, but we have found these to be appropriate for our customers and their comfort.

To measure the broomcorn, place a long strip of blue painter's tape onto a tabletop with markings at 0 inches, 22 inches, 28 inches, and 34 inches. Some crafters make a story stick by taking a long piece of wood or a yardstick and making permanent marks on it instead of using tape on a table. The story stick can be saved for future broomcorn sorting, whereas the tape needs to be reapplied every time you need it.

Next, lay a piece of broomcorn on the tape or story stick with the knuckle (where the hurl meets the stem) at the 0 inches mark. See where the tip of the broomcorn hits on your tape or story stick and place it in the appropriate bucket. Sometimes the tip will hit exactly on a mark. If this happens, use your judgment to determine which bucket to put it into. Most of the broomcorn will fall into the middle two buckets.

Image #6: Piece of broom straw measured with buckets

That's it; you're done sorting!

Prepare the Hurl

If you ordered hurl, the material will arrive bound in large bundles. Many broom makers leave it in these bundles and pull out what they need when they need it. We find that technique to be messy and frustrating and prefer to divvy it up into 4-ounce bunches, as most brooms can be made in multiples of 4 ounces. Making a kitchen broom? Pull six bunches. Making a whisk? Pull two bunches, and so on.

Preparation is much simpler for hurl than craft broomcorn. You will need an electric kitchen scale, a jar or container to hold the broomcorn as it is being weighed, and small rubber bands.

To weigh, first zero out your scale and select ounce measurements. Collect a bunch of hurl in your hand that you can wrap your fingers around, thumb touching your middle finger. This will give you a starting point. Weigh that bunch, then add or subtract pieces of hurl until you get to 4 ounces. A single piece of hurl can change the weight, but it is up to you as to how particular you want to be. Secure your bunch with a rubber band and store your bunches upright in buckets or boxes.

Now that we have discussed the materials used in the craft of broom making, we are ready to look into the tools needed. Like the materials, the tools are relatively inexpensive and easy to obtain. Next, we'll look into those materials and explore what they are and how they are used to create your custom besom.

Chapter 4
The Tools

In this book, we will be using tools that are usually easy to buy or make and are the tools that we use in our own crafting. There are other tools and machines in the broom maker's closet that are helpful but certainly not necessary. Most of those tools are hard to find, as they are no longer made. For the most part, they are found as antiques and are quite rare, though there are some broom makers who are starting to make new ones. We only use what is listed here because simplicity is one of our favorite parts about this craft.

Broom Needle

Another specialized tool that is easy to purchase online is the broom needle. The broom needle is required to stitch the brush of the broom into a round or flat shape depending on the type of broom you are making. Broom needles come in a variety of styles, but we prefer a flat, wide needle with a sharp, single point because we find that it glides through the broomcorn more easily and we don't have to learn any special techniques to use it. Be sure to use care with the needle; the tip is sharp, and you may hurt yourself if you aren't paying attention.

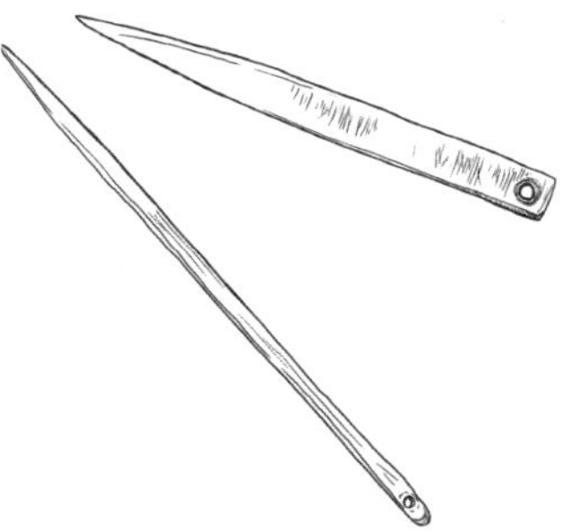

Image #7: Broom needles

Foot Spinner

The most specialized tool that we use is a foot spinner, which is easy to make with basic woodworking skills, but there are a few broom makers who are manufacturing and selling them online. The foot spinner keeps the twine off the ground, keeping it clean, and reduces wear and tear of the twine, preventing breakage while working with it. The foot spinner is not essential though; many broom makers and broom making students use a simple 1 × 2-inch board cut to approximately 28 inches, or a 2-inch diameter dowel about 28 inches long with a single ¼-inch hole drilled at the middle point to tie your twine to.

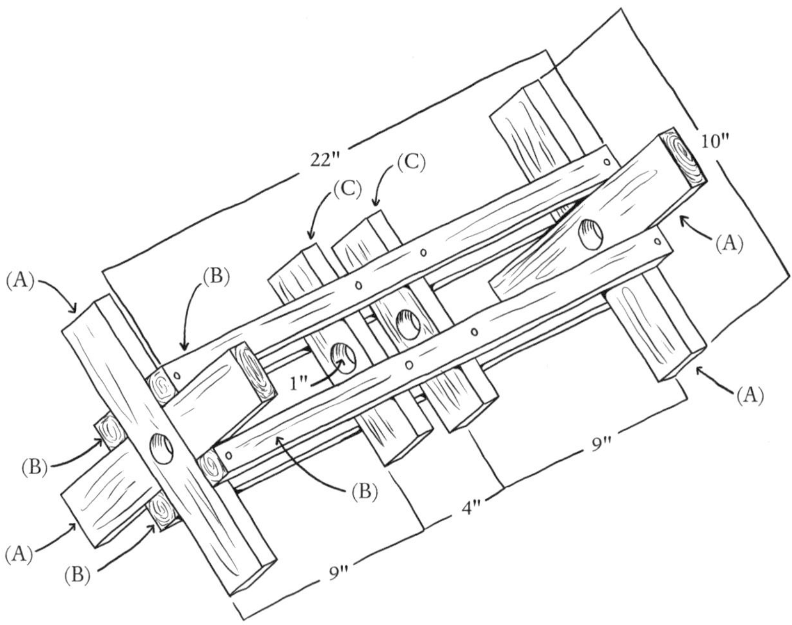

MATERIALS LIST				
PART	L	W	th	Qty
A	10"	2"	¾"	4
B	22"	1"	1"	4
C	7"	2"	¾"	2

Image #8: Spinner diagram

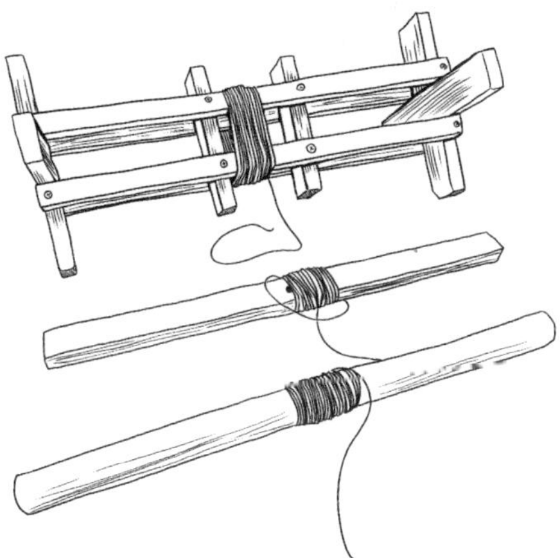

Image #9: Spinner and alternatives

Jerk String

In order to secure the end of the nylon when wrapping, we use a jerk string to pull the end of the twine through the final wraps instead of using a knot. A jerk string is simply a piece of nylon twine about 12 inches long, singed at each end to prevent fraying. The jerk string can wear out after a few uses, so save your nylon twine cut-offs to make more so that you'll always have one available.

Lighter

Since the nylon twine we use for wraps and weaving is made from twisted plastic, a lighter is used to melt the cut ends to keep it from unraveling. Note that the melted plastic at the end of the twine is very hot! Give it a few seconds to cool off and harden up before you touch it.

Stitching Clamp

This is a specialized tool used to flatten the brush of the broom in preparation for stitching it flat.

Activity: Make a Stitching Clamp

These materials can be purchased from a hardware store:

- 2 pieces of smooth 1 × 2-inch lumber, 10 inches long
- 2 ¼-inch × 2-inch-long bolts with two matching wing nuts

These are the tools you will need:

- Ruler
- Electric drill
- ⅜-inch drill bit

Step 1: Using your ruler, make a mark at every 1-inch interval along both boards.

Step 2: Using the ⅜-inch drill bit, drill a hole at every mark on both boards.

Step 3: Put the two boards together so the holes line up. Insert the bolts into the boards in two places. Attach the wing nuts.

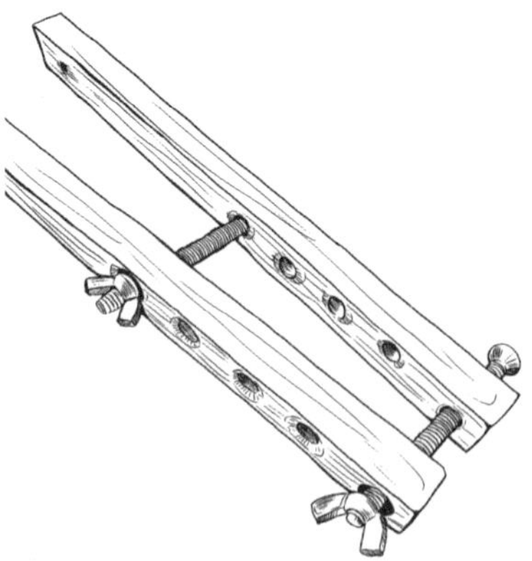

Image #10: Stitching clamp

Scissors

We use standard 8-inch multipurpose scissors to trim the bottom of the broomcorn to the desired shape and length. Broomcorn is very hard on the scissor's cutting edges though, so don't use anything delicate. You will be using a lot of pressure to cut the broomcorn—please keep your fingers away from the blades!

Utility Knife, Box Cutter, or Broom Knife

The stems will need to be cut, and the ends of the broomcorn will need to be trimmed. There are a few options here. The utility knife or box cutter can be purchased from any hardware store. The broom knife is a specialized knife that can be ordered online. Every broom maker has their own preference for which knife to use. We use a box cutter most of the time due to its easy accessibility and the ability to replace worn-down blades with fresh, sharp ones. Like the broom needle, whatever type of knife you use, it must be sharp enough to cut through the broomcorn, which means it will be more than sharp enough to cut through you. Always cut in the direction away from you and your body!

Velcro Strap

With some broom types, the brush of the broomcorn can get unwieldy as you are working with it. In order to control the brush, wrap it tightly with a Velcro strap. Any width of strap will do as long as it can go around the brush. You can buy hook and loop tape—or better known by its brand name, Velcro—at any major home improvement store in a roll that you can cut to your desired length, or you can buy straps premade.

Chapter 5
Basic Techniques

Once you've acquired your tools and prepared your materials, there are some setup procedures and basic techniques that you need to know before starting. These fundamentals will allow you to create a strong and usable broom.

Your Workspace

The first thing to do is figure out where you will be building your broom. Find an open space with a minimum of 3 feet on either side of you and 3 feet in front of you. You will have quite a bit of broomcorn trimmings on the ground when you are finished, so be sure the floor is easy to sweep. Be aware that it is difficult to vacuum broomcorn, even with a shop vac. You will need a comfortable and sturdy chair and a table that you can easily reach while seated. Things don't have to be fancy; we use an old wing chair and an old school desk that we found. Make sure the area is well lit.

Remember, posture is important in this craft. Keep yourself in an upright seated position; it is very easy to slouch while building your broom, and that will result in a sore back and shoulders. Keep your arms close to your body and your elbows at a comfortable angle to reduce strain on your shoulders and arms.

Setup Procedures

In broom making, everything that you do—from winding the twine onto the spinner to pulling the jerk string at the end—is geared for keeping tension on the twine as you work. Without strong tension, your broom will fall apart.

Prepare Your Spindle

Wind your nylon twine around the middle of a foot spinner, dowel, or piece of wood. Each type of broom requires a different amount of twine, and we have indicated an approximate length you will need with our broom recipes. It is always better, however, to wrap more twine than you think you will need because each broom is made from a single strand of twine, and it is not easy to tie or splice your twine in the middle of your session. Don't overfill your spinner, however, because the nylon will have an opportunity to stretch too much or wear down, so we only put enough twine on our spinners for two or three brooms.

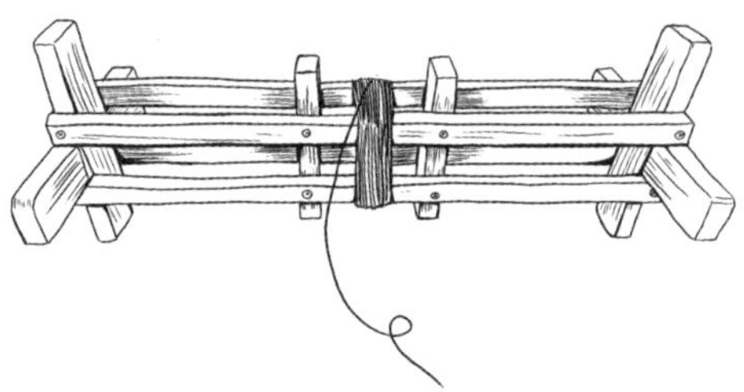

Image #11: Wound foot spindle with twine

Set Up Your Workstation

Next, set up your workstation. Remember that you will need to be able to keep your tools and materials within easy reach of your chair, as you will not be able to get up once you get started.

Have a seat and hold the stick in your lap with the top, where the hanging loop hole is, to your right and the tapered bottom to your left. It doesn't matter which is your dominant hand. Place the spinner in front of you and stretch your legs out so that your heels are resting on the floor. Put the spinner under your feet, one on either side of the twine. You will be controlling the spinner using your feet, which will provide the tension needed to make a strong broom. Pull the end of the twine to you, making sure the twine is going over the top of the spinner toward you. Keep your feet on the spinner, slightly lifting them to allow the spinner to release more twine, then replacing them to stop it.

Set Up Your Stick

Thread the end of the twine through the small hole at the bottom of the stick. Tie a knot around the handle to keep it from coming out. Roll the stick toward you so that the twine goes over the top of the stick. When you get the twine all the way around the stick, it will equal one wrap. Wrap the stick three times, working toward the bottom of the stick.

Use your feet to always keep tension on the twine, releasing more only as needed. Turn, pull, turn, pull...The twine should be kept taut enough at all times to "sing" when plucked. You will feel the twine stretch just slightly but not break. Be aware that if the twine breaks, it will snap back toward you and that hurts, but all broom makers have done it by accident at least once.

As mentioned previously, tension is the most important part of broom making. There should be enough tension placed on the twine that it creates a little divot in the broomcorn, securing it in place. Without this tension, the broom will fall apart with use, and that's not what we're aiming for.

Stitching Techniques

Stitching is the critical step in finishing a broom. How you stitch your broom determines the final shape it will have and how effective it will be as a cleaning instrument, and strong stitching strengthens and secures the broomcorn. Early brooms were stitched in the round, but in the early nineteenth century, the Shakers developed a way to flatten the broom, thus making it more efficient as a cleaning tool due to its greater floor surface area and compacted brush. Witch brooms are most commonly round, but they certainly don't have to be!

Most broom makers estimate the amount of 7- or 9-ply thread needed to stitch a broom by arm lengths because it is quick and easy. We're sure there are some who use specific measurements, but we have not met any. Hold the tip of the thread in your hand and point your arm straight out beside you. The distance from your hand to your nose is one arm length. The type and size of broom will determine how many arm lengths are needed to complete the stitching. You don't want to run out of thread in the middle of your work, so pull off some extra just in case.

Approximate lengths are as follows for the broom recipes in this book:

Cobwebber: 1.5 arm lengths
Hearth broom: 2 arm lengths
Kitchen brooms: 3 arm lengths
Turkey wing whisk: 1.5 arm lengths
Hawk tail whisk: 1.5 arm lengths

Round Stitching

Pull off the amount of thread you will need to complete your stitching. Thread the thread through your single-pointed needle and tie a knot at the end.

Image #12: Round hide the knot

Insert the needle into the brush just below the bottom of the stick, coming out the opposite side. We'll call this point the twelve o'clock position. Pull the thread only enough so that the knot gets embedded into the brush.

Wrap the thread around the brush three times, pulling tightly, bringing all of the broomcorn together. Looking from the top of the broom down the handle, insert your needle above the wraps at the twelve o'clock position and exit the needle directly opposite (straight through), above the wraps, at the six o'clock position.

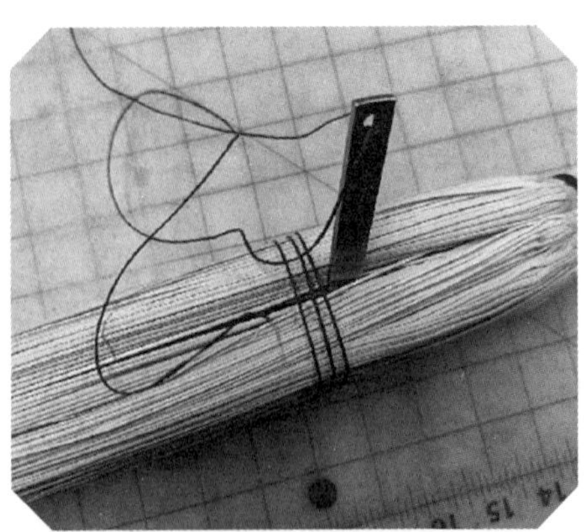

Image #13: Round first 12 to 6

Insert the needle directly below the wraps at the six o'clock position and exit at the two o'clock position below the wraps.

Insert the needle directly where the thread exited above the wraps at the two o'clock position and exit at the eight o'clock position above the wraps.

Insert the needle directly below the wraps at the eight o'clock position and exit at the four o'clock position below the wraps.

Insert the needle directly where the thread exited above the wraps at the four o'clock position and exit at the ten o'clock position above the wraps.

Insert the needle directly below where the thread exited at the ten o'clock position and exit directly below the wraps at the twelve o'clock position.

Tie a knot in the thread approximately ½ inch from where the thread exited. Insert the needle directly above the wraps at the twelve o'clock position and exit at any point opposite, pulling the knot into the broom.

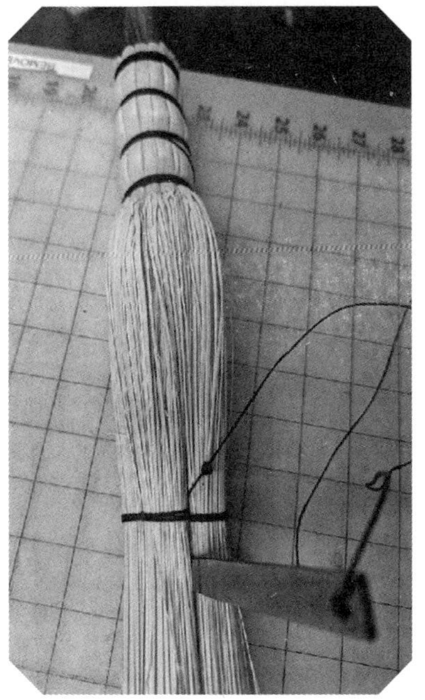

Image #14: Round knot at 12

Cut the thread as close to the brush as possible. Use the needle to push the end of the thread back into the broom to hide it.

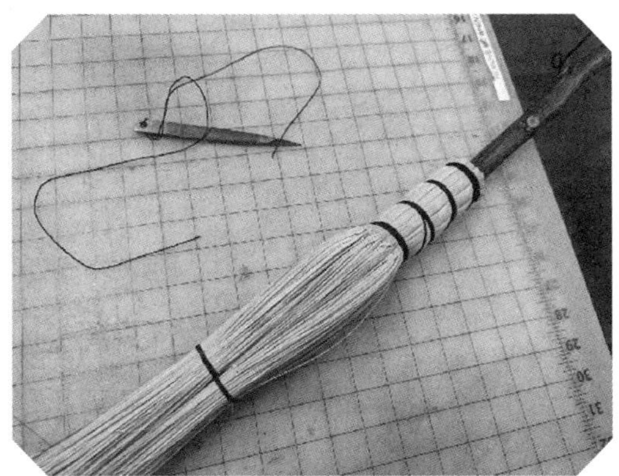

Image #15: Round finished

Flat Stitching Technique

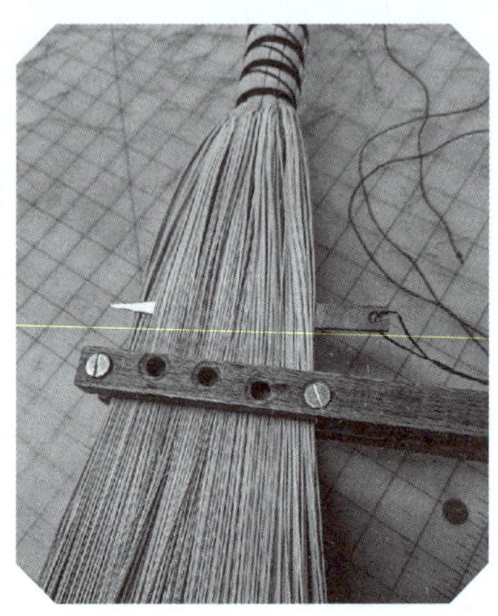

Image #16: First needle entry

After your broom has fully dried from the process of adding the brush, clamp the broom into the vise approximately 2 inches toward the brush from the bottom of the handle, below the point at the bottom of the stick inside the broom. This will flatten the brush. Be sure the clamp is laying in line with the sides of the broom so that it will lay or hang flat. Pull off the amount of waxed linen thread necessary for the type of broom you are making. Tie a knot at the end of the thread and put the thread through the hole on the needle.

Insert the needle between the stick and vise, just below the vise in the side of the broom and exit about ½ inch from the opposite side. Pull the knot into the brush, hiding it.

Wrap the thread around the brush four times below the clamp. Insert the needle where the thread came out above the wraps and exit the needle on the opposite side above the wraps.

Insert the needle directly below the wraps, exiting on the opposite side below the wraps.

Insert the needle directly above the wraps and exit about ¾ inch away from the previous stitch, above the wraps. Pull tightly.

Image #17: First stitch front

Insert the needle immediately below the wraps and exit directly opposite, below the wraps.

Repeat the previous two steps for as many times as it takes to go across your broom.

On the last stitch after exiting the broom, tie a knot approximately ¾ inch from where the thread exited the broom. Insert the needle directly below and exit about halfway across the broom, pulling the knot into the broom to hide it.

Image #18: First shift stitch

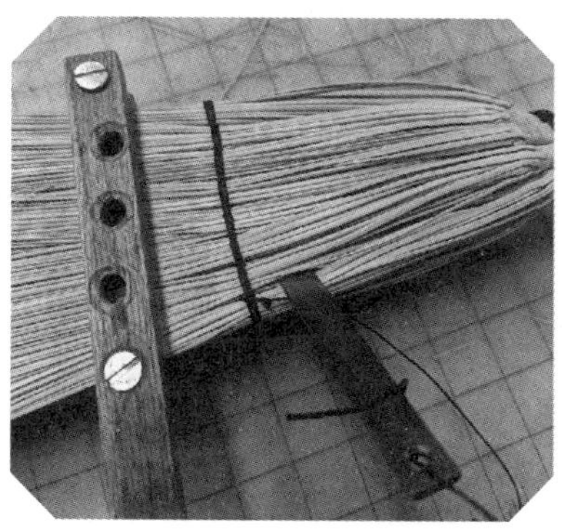

Image #19: Knotted end

Cut the thread as close to the brush as possible. Use your needle to push the end back into the broom to hide it.

You can make as many rows of stitching as you like depending on the size of the broom and the effect you desire. We usually make two to three rows per broom and one row on whisks (if we choose to stitch them at all).

Image #20: Finished stitching

Tying Off

When you have finished weaving the top of your broom, there is a fun little trick to tying off the twine so that it doesn't unravel. As with everything in broom making, the key is to keep everything as taut as possible throughout the process.

When you reach the end of your weave, fold the jerk string in half and place it under the twine with the loop facing away from the weaving. For example, if you're working toward the right, put the string in so that the loop is to the right.

Use your left thumbnail to hold the twine down tightly. Use a lighter to cut the twine about 6 inches away from the jerk string. Your thumbnail should prevent any loss of tension when the twine is cut.

Thread the melted cut end of the twine through the loop of the jerk string.

Hold the cut end of the twine with your right hand, maintaining tension. With a sharp motion using your left hand, yank the jerk string to the left, pulling the cut end of the twine underneath the wraps, securing it. If your tension is right, this can be difficult. Feel free to use a pair of pliers to help.

Use your knife to cut the twine as close to the wraps as possible without cutting the wraps themselves.

Image #21: Folded jerk string

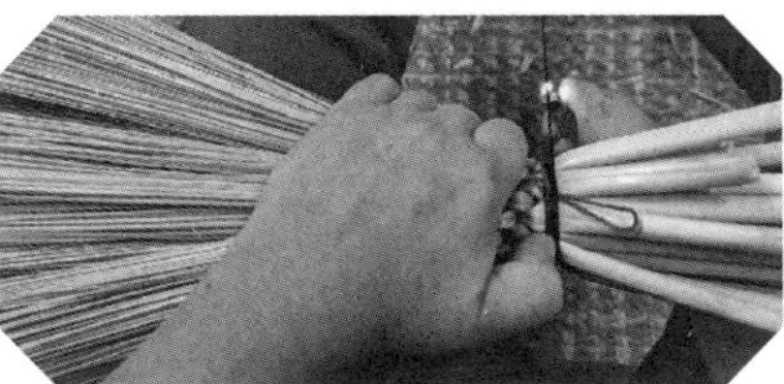
Image #22: Using thumb to hold tension

Image #23: Cut end of twine through the jerk string loop

Image #24: Pulling the jerk string

Image #25: Jerk string after it has been pulled under wraps

Image #26: Trimming the twine

Chapter 6
Getting to Know Your Broom

Many of us have had a broom for most of our magical lives. We asked some witches about their brooms, and many couldn't tell us where theirs came from or how they acquired it. However, they were certain they'd had it for a while. A few thought they inherited it; some believed they were gifted it. One person told us they thought their ex left it and it was handy, and one older woman made hers years ago for a Halloween party and just started using it.

The bottom line is, it doesn't matter at this point where you acquired the broom you currently have. However, for those of you who have just found or made a broom of your own, or for those whose broom is getting weary and broken down, here are some tips and rituals to help you.

Consecrating Your Broom

Any new magical tool is a joy to acquire. How many have felt the thrill of making a new wand? Or of either forging or being gifted a new ritual knife? Finding the perfect cauldron or ritual garb? And we all enjoy new garb when we are able to get some. A new broom is no different in that respect; however, there are some rituals that you may want to be aware of before you try to use the new broom in circle magically. In fact, we would suggest you do something like this for every new tool you acquire if you do not already. Let's be prudent here. Magical safety is paramount in our Craft.

The following ritual is based loosely on traditional Wiccan consecration rituals. Alter per your own practice.

Preparation

When setting up the ritual circle, place the new broom in the center of the altar, if you use one, or a designated space that is clean and readily available. After all, it's the star of the show, right? Once the altar is set up and those participating have gathered, you can begin your ritual. Keep in mind that you don't need an audience for this ritual if you don't wish for one. Consecrating your broom is a personal activity; however, some witches like to have others there to celebrate the acceptance of the new broom into the arsenal of tools, especially if it is to be used by all.

Materials Needed

- The broom
- An herb or grass that you use for cleansing to be burned
- A dish of some kind that is nonflammable to place the burned herbs after smoke cleansing
- A fire instrument, such as matches
- A fire suppressant

Directions

Open the circle from the east per your tradition or however you are comfortable. East is the quarter of new beginnings. The sun rises every day from the east to give light to the world and power to those who know how to use it. Consecrating a new broom is another example of new beginnings for both you and the broom.

Once back at the altar, smoke cleanse the broom with whatever herbs you or your coven use. Some witches use dried lavender, mint, or even cannabis. Use whatever it is you are most comfortable with and is also legal. Allow the smoke from the herbs to waft up to the broom. You may also use fresh water and lightly sprinkle the broom to remove negative energies. At the same time, say, "This broom is a tool. This broom is [my/] our tool. This broom may assist [me/us] in both [my/our] daily and magical duties. [I/we] shall care for this broom as all [my/our] other magical tools. [I/we] accept this broom and ask that it accept [me/us]."

Next, starting at east again, present the broom, saying, "This is [my/our] broom. I introduce [my/our] broom to the east for your recognition for future rituals. Accept this broom as you have accepted [me/us]." Next, move to the south and repeat the words, replacing the quarter name. Do the same for the west and north.

Once back at the altar, place the broom back where you had it. Turn to the center of the circle and say, "[I/we] have accepted this broom as [my/our] magical tool to assist [me/us] in all [my/our] magical and daily duties. [I/we] shall keep this tool secure as long as it is with [me/us]."

From the east and going counterclockwise, close the circle as you would in your manner or in a way that is comfortable, and thank the quarters for being there for you. Remind them that the broom is a magical tool and an extension of your hand as a wand or knife would be, and the broom is a tool to be used.

Sabbats, Esbats, and Full Moons

In traditional Wicca and other similar traditions, a sabbat, esbat, or full moon ritual begins when the high priest, priestess, or priestx takes the broom from the altar and sweeps the circle, removing any excess energies from previous work done there or any negative energies that may have accumulated. After that, the high priest, priestess, or priestx may open the circle in their specific tradition with a wand or knife. If you are used to those traditions, then carry out whatever your particular path requires. However, you can choose to instead use the broom to open and close the circle. Here are some easy steps to follow.

Preparation

When setting up your circle and altar prior to ritual, place the broom on the altar as you would your knife or wand. When ready for the ritual, take the broom from the altar. You may hold the broom either horizontally or vertically. The broom doesn't mind either way, and some may not be able to hold the broom steady enough horizontally to make it completely around the circle. Let's face it: Some of us have been doing this for many years, and we are not as young, strong, and spry as we used to be.

Materials Needed

- The broom
- Whatever altar or ritual tools you use in your specific path or tradition
- If you are calling quarters, then quarter altars and whatever you wish for those quarters

Directions

Walk the broom around the circle in a clockwise manner, presenting the broom to the four quarters and honoring the quarters with the broom as you would with a wand. If you choose to speak at these quarters, then you may say something like, "I use this broom to open the path of [whichever quarter you are at]. This broom is an extension of my will and my power and shall represent my course through this rite."

Once back at the altar, state the purpose of the ritual. Are you sweeping away something or sweeping something in? It's important to articulate what your intention is during the ritual so as not to confuse any deities who might be listening, and the broom would like to know what is expected of it also.

At that point, begin sweeping the circle in a clockwise manner, beginning at whatever point is appropriate. As you sweep, with every motion, repeat what you are trying to sweep out or in. If you are sweeping something away, then sweep with a deliberate motion outward. Say something such as, "I sweep [whatever] out of [my life/wherever you wish the item to be dismissed from.]" If you are sweeping something into your life, then change up your statement a little: "I sweep [whatever] into [my life/wherever you wish the requested item to arrive]."

Again, as we will say many times, be articulate about your intention and purpose. Before ritual, practice what you are going to say and how you will say it. The gods are literal in their understanding of humans, and even though we are their servants and, at times, friends, they are still often capricious and will on a whim grant you what you ask for even if it is not what you meant.

Once back at the altar, thank the broom. A simple verbal thank you is sufficient. It doesn't even need to be loud enough to be heard by anyone other than the broom. This is an important part of every broom ritual, not just those for sabbats or esbats. The broom has done all the work. All you've done is carry it around the circle and muttered a few words. The broom was the conduit between this realm and the ethereal one.

When you are done with the rest of the ritual workings, you will close the circle with the broom. Take the broom again and go back to the quarters in a counterclockwise direction, releasing the quarters in the presence of the broom and acknowledging their assistance in the ritual. As with the gods, you don't want to anger the quarters. Once back at the altar, place the broom on the altar.

After the ritual, retrieve your tools from the altar and make certain the broom is cleaned of debris before placing it back in its place of honor in your house. You may clean the broom by shaking it out at the ritual site to loosen any physical debris. Then take some fresh water and sprinkle the broom lightly to finish the cleansing. Don't sprinkle too much. You don't want the broom wet because it may mildew. Just as you don't want to carry dirt or negative energy into your house with your shoes or clothing, you do not want to carry such things back to your house with your broom.

Optional:

If you are celebrating a specific sabbat, try using a broom with a wood associated with that sabbat. Here is a list:

1. Imbolc, February 1–2: Maple
2. Ostara, March 19–22: Ash, elm
3. Beltane, May 1: Oak, birch
4. Litha/Midsummer, June 20–21: Holly
5. Lughnasadh/Lammas, August 1: Maple
6. Mabon, September 22–23: Any fruit tree; apple or cherry are very good
7. Samhain, October 31: Black walnut
8. Yule, December 21–22: Holly, yew, and pine

Retiring a Broom from Active Service

Everything wears out. Cars, people, even mountains eventually wear down. Therefore, it's not too much of a stretch to understand that your broom is going to get old and start to fall apart. Now, you can repair an old broom.

Doing so is similar to building one. But you may not want to. The broom may be too old, too damaged, or too tired to perform its duties anymore.

An important note is to never consecrate a new broom before you retire the old one. If you plan on keeping the old broom, cleanse it, and give it a place of honor in your home. This way you have not disgraced the service of the old broom—the senior broom—before bringing in the new one. It is just bad manners to consecrate a new one first.

Preparation

Whether you plan to repair or retire your broom, you should first remove whatever energy is in the broom. Residual energy can be problematic when repairing a broom, for the energies may not want the broom repaired. With clean fresh water, sprinkle the broom and say, "I cleanse you from all energies, positive or dark. I release you from all responsibilities that were yours and allow you to begin again."

At this point, if you are going to repair and reuse the broom, do so and then reconsecrate the broom as though it was a new broom. If you choose not to use it anymore, continue to follow this ritual to retire the senior broom. Note that you may also use this ritual to retire any other items you no longer use or that are beyond repair.

We know covens that have a fire circle once a year to burn all the things they no longer use or are useful. Some things that go in the fire are old candles, notebooks of spells that are no longer wanted, lesson plans that are outdated—whatever. The following ritual is based on that tradition. But you must be cautious, though, that the broom is not synthetic. It is very dangerous to burn anything, but to burn plastic-bristled brooms or other artificial substances is asking for trouble.

Further, do not burn anything in a confined space or indoors. Make certain you have an open circle with good ventilation and fire suppression available should things get out of hand.

Materials Needed

- The broom to be retired
- A firepit or large fireproof cauldron or container; it must be big enough to burn the broom

- Some form of fire suppression in case of emergencies
- A fire ignition tool such as matches
- Whatever else you ritualistically use in a circle or ritual

Directions

Retiring your broom is done in circle. It doesn't have to be a special day or night to cast a circle. Similar to consecrating a new broom, you just need a circle to show respect to the broom and alert the quarters, or however you call circle, that this broom is no longer your tool. If a circle is not in your tradition, then create sacred space as you normally would and retire the broom there.

Place your broom on the altar. Once the broom is in place, cast the circle clockwise from west. West is the quarter of endings. As the day ends in the west, so will this circle and this tool.

Once the circle is cast, take the broom and talk to it. Remember, you've possibly been with this broom longer than some of your coven mates or friends, and it's been with you through good and not-so-good times. Thank the broom for all the service it's given you and wish the broom luck as it goes to teach new brooms before they are grown and made. Magical tools have feelings. If you don't believe that, then you've never tried to get a wand to work after you've abused it by leaving it out for the cat to play with or let your athame rust and then wonder why you keep cutting yourself in circle. Actions have consequences.

Take the broom around the circle clockwise starting at west. Stop at each quarter and say: "This broom has been with [me/us] for [X years], [X rituals], and [whatever other functions there were]. In honor of the service, [I/we] give it back to nature to teach the next generation of straw and wood."

Back at the altar, place the broom in the unlit firepit. As you carefully light the ritual fire, say, "This broom was [my/our] friend and [my/our] tool. [I/we] part with this broom to allow it to go forward and teach others yet to come."

Light the firepit. As the broom burns, think about what you have accomplished with this broom, what you have been through, and what you would not have been able to do if it had not been for this wonderful tool.

Once the entire broom has been reduced to ash, you may close the circle. From west and going counterclockwise, thank the quarters for attending this ritual and for assisting you in sending your broom onward.

If you are so inclined, you may consecrate your new broom during the same night, but don't have both out at the same time. Treat the new broom with the same reverence as the old one, and you should be fine.

Chapter 7
Brooms in Ritual and Magic

This chapter will discuss the rituals you may need or want for your circle, your house, or your magic path. This list is not all-inclusive. Use this as a starting point. Write in the margins or the blank spaces. Fill this book with your thoughts, successes, and failures.

Now, we will share when to use the brooms in specific rituals. We will show you which ritual is best for which broom, or the other way around, depending on how you wish to look at it.

The House Broom

We like to keep our houses clean. Many of us have vacuum cleaners or, more recently, the things that run around the floor pulling up all the dust that most of us would rather forget about. Some of us, though, use a broom. And that broom, whether metal, wood, plastic, or other material, constitutes your house broom.

When Gypsey was a child in the 1950s, her family had a Fuller Brush man. He would come to the house about every six months and sell cleaning supplies, dustpans, and brooms. She still has one of the original metal dustpans out in the shop. A few years ago, a friend of hers who made brooms gifted her a house broom. It looked like all the other brooms you see in the stores, but this one was a *real* broom. There were no plastic or metal parts. The bristles were broomstraw, like the ones detailed in this book, and the cleaning was amazing.

The moral to this story is that just because something is no longer easy to find or easy to purchase doesn't mean it's no longer worth the trouble to find it. Unfortunately, Fuller Brush has succumbed to the way of plastic and metal. But good brooms are still available out there, and they are worth the effort to find. But what happens when you do find the house broom you are looking for? As with all the other uses of brooms in this chapter, there is a right and less-than-right way to introduce a broom to your magical house.

After you acquire the broom, we recommend you introduce it to your house. If this is to be your house broom and it is the one you will use to actually clean and sweep your floors, then you need to identify it as such. It does no good to lead the broom to believe it's going to be a ritual broom and then hang it in a closet or the laundry room. All brooms have duties.

While some people may be adept at doing two diametrically opposed things equally well, brooms are not those things. If you want a broom to be used in circle, then keep it for circle. If you want it to be used to clean your house, then use it to clean your house. Be honest with the broom up front. Once acquired, tell the broom that you will use it to keep the house clean—that the function of cleanliness is essential to good magic, and the broom is an important part of your magical tool kit by being able to sweep effectively.

Show the broom around the house. Talk to the broom as you sweep the first time. All magical tools have abilities, and by now you should fully understand that the tools also have wants and needs, even though they may not be able to articulate them as humans or others do. Also, this broom is as important as all your other brooms, so clean it after use and give it a safe and secure place to hang. We both keep our house brooms in the laundry room on special hooks. Gypsey's broom has been with her for a number of years and looks as good as when she acquired it because she cares.

Our ancestors had limited time, money, and resources. They acquired things at a cost either to themselves or to their families and kept the items in good or as good working order for as long as possible. Gypsey's grandfather had a saying when she was growing up that she heard many times in other households as well: "Buy it new. Wear it out. Make it do. Or do without." We could afford to spend more time making it do in this day and age. Planned obsolescence may be good for the manufacturers that make poorly constructed items to be used up quickly, but it does us, the consumer, no good at the house level. Remember that when you acquire your house broom. It can be with you for most of your life if you treat it well and care for it properly.

There are a few types of woods that do not make good house brooms. We do not recommend black walnut, datura, ebony, padauk, or poison ivy. The better ones are holly, willow, privet, and any fruit wood because the wood smells nice. Whatever wood you do choose, make certain that you start off by telling the broom it is a house broom. That's just common courtesy.

The Travel Broom

We all travel. Some of us travel more than others. When Gypsey was in the military, she was almost always on the road or in the air. She averaged a permanent move every nine months for seven years. That's a lot of travel time.

During that period, she didn't have many magical tools with her. Soldiers, even officers, lived in tents, temporary quarters, and small apartments. Overseas, she often had a house cleaner and ate at the Officer's Mess or the Commanding General's Mess. Someone else did her laundry and her dusting. Therefore, she never needed a travel broom.

Now that she's older and travels less, she has the luxury of having a magical kit that goes with her. And part of that kit is a small broom for such purposes. Some would call the broom a whisk broom. Others might say it's a dust broom. Still more would use the term *short handled.* Whatever they call it, it's a travel broom because it travels with you and it works for you as well. In the next section of this book, we will discuss how to make whisks. They are almost identical to full-sized brooms, but they aren't full sized. Everything about them is in miniature. They are shorter, lighter, smaller, and more compact. They are easier to take with you for rituals and spellwork on the road. But believe us when we tell you they still pack a punch when you need it.

When you first acquire a travel broom, show it your travel kit. Explain to the broom what it is to be used for. Is it for cleaning your spaces while away or is it a ritual broom to replace its bigger sibling? You may wish to perform a short circle to initiate the broom, perhaps in the driveway since that's the place it will be departing from and arriving to. We recommend a small pouch for the broom, perhaps sewn by you either by hand or machine, to keep the broom clean during travel and protect the bristles. But if you choose not to, then make certain you pack it well to keep it from being damaged.

Finally, when you use it at hotels or festivals, treat it as a full-sized broom. The power of a whisk is equal to any other broom and will give you good results if you treat it well and with respect. Remember, this is a broom that you will have for some time and possibly pass down to your next generation.

Whisk brooms may be made from almost any wood available, even datura, padauk, or poison ivy, depending on what energy you are requiring and what function the broom is being asked to perform.

Divination with Your Broom

We talked earlier about a broom being a really big wand with a bushy end. And to that end, a broom may do all that a wand does. And if you believe in size mattering, then the broom will do it supersized. Just like a wand, a broom is a great tool for divining your path or the path of others if you are so able to do that.

Two very good woods for divination are laurel and sycamore. Laurel is easy to find, and there are many types of laurels to work with. We like to make brooms from sycamore due to the grain pattern.

Materials Needed

- A white candle
- A chair
- A table for the candle
- An ignition instrument to light the candle
- A form of fire suppression
- The broom

Preparation

When divining with a broom, it's the same as divining with a wand. Find a quiet place large enough to house you, the broom, a space for circle, and a safe table for a candle. You may or may not choose to set up wards and call the quarters. We always call quarters any time we cast a circle, but we know others who will jump right into the circle and talk to the quarters as they pass them. Some don't call quarters at all. It is always up to you and the path or tradition you follow.

Inside the circle, if you cast one, place a comfortable chair at the southeastern point between east and south. Ideally, you want the eastern light behind you. Just realize that east is the quarter of beginning. Place the candle across from you on a small table at the northwestern half quarter. You will be sitting in the chair at the southeast half quarter looking at the candle in the northwest half quarter.

Directions

Dim or extinguish as many lights as you safely can. Leave enough light to move about the circle, or if you wish, use a hand torch or small candle that you can shut off or snuff once you are ready to begin.

Light a white candle on the table. Sit in the chair and shut off all lights. Place the broom in your lap with the bristles facing southwest. Gently hold the broom on your lap with your two hands and look at the candle.

You may verbally articulate or mentally articulate your question or your query toward the light. As you think of what you wish to know, remember to say or think that this is done with the permission of all concerned and is not to be used to harm, bind, or banish anyone or anything.

Continue to stare at the candle, going deeper and deeper into the light until you are granted access to what you are seeking. Also remember to leave a door open behind you in your concentration for your exit. While it is rare that you may become bound by the light, stranger things have happened. Once you have completed your divination, clear your mind and thank any deities that assisted you along the way.

Stand up and walk over to the candle. Snuff it out. Then turn back on or relight whatever lights you had and, with the broom, close the circle, thanking all the quarters and half quarters for attending and assisting. You have completed the divination ritual with your broom.

Handfasting

It is a great and joyous thing to find the love of your life. And once you have found that one you wish to spend your life with, this is where the handfasting ritual comes in.

Each tradition has its own philosophy of when and how to handfast. Most (but not all, so don't say we're being definitive in this) of those who plan on such an endeavor will wait a year and a day from the time they meet to the time they handfast. And many couples we know then make the handfasting for a year and a day as a trial run. Again, dating someone and being head over heels in love with that person will change drastically at times once you are living together and cooking, eating, paying bills, and sleeping in the same habitat.

Therefore, the ritual of handfasting is a fluid one. There is no hard and locked-down script for this. As in any wedding ceremony, the couple plan their event, evaluate the options, and, after all the data is in, pull the trigger. Or…they just jump the broom in the backyard in a fit of passion and throw all caution to the winds. It can go either way. Most handfasting, though, will utilize a broom.

Choosing the correct broom for the ritual is important. If you want your joining to be strong and solid, then you choose oak. If you are in love (who isn't at this point?) you might choose cherry. Or if you are doing this out of desperation for security and protection, then there is always the nuclear option, and you can go dark and pick one of the less-positive woods. No matter the choice you make, it will always be yours, and it should always remain your choice. Weddings, funerals, and other personal moments in your life are yours—not your family's, your friends', or some stranger's you found on the internet.

The following ritual is given from the perspective of the priest, priestess, or priestx. Adapt as needed.

Materials Needed

- A broom
- A blanket to place the broom on
- Tools and other supplies required for ritual circle, per your tradition
- Handfasting decor and post-ritual refreshments, as desired

Preparation

First, clean the ritual space. Have everything ready when the couple and guests arrive.

Set out refreshments if that is what is chosen for after the ceremony.

Directions

First, call the circle if that is your tradition. If you do, you'll want to use the broom that you are going to jump. After that is complete, place the broom on the ground, preferably on a blanket or some other protective surface. Keep the broom clean from all outside energies.

Call the couple into the circle area between you and the broom. We've seen the high priestess, priestx, or priest stand with the broom facing them or parallel to them. That decision is theirs as a couple or yours as a leader.

Pick up the broom from the ground and sweep the circle starting from the east, the quarter of all beginnings, in a clockwise direction. As you sweep, make certain you sweep out and that when you recock the broom for the next sweep, you don't inadvertently sweep something back in. The recock is when you pull the broom to the back height of the sweep and then momentarily stop before descending to the floor again. Think of how rowers turn their oars when they pull back for the next dip and pull.

Once you have completed the sweeping, hand the broom to the couple and have each of them sweep the circle as you did, one and then the other. The order of who does it first doesn't matter.

After all three of you have swept the circle, return the broom to the ground and say whatever you or they planned. Vows, as with all else, are personal. The couple should write them and then speak them to each other as one would in any other wedding ceremony.

After they have done such, you may then say something if that is wished. Finally, as in other rituals of marriage, ask the coven or guests in the circle if they would like to say something fitting about the couple. This is not the place for guests to spout off about how awful one or the other is or how they shouldn't be handfasted. That ship sailed with the tide a long time ago. This is a time of celebration not a drunken or anger-laced diatribe.

Finally, instruct the couple to join hands and either step over or jump over the broom. Once the broom has been "jumped," present the couple to the gathering with some positive wording. Again, this is your chance to send them on their way to a hopefully long life together.

Before you dismiss the couple, recover the broom from the ground and sweep once more from the east in a counterclockwise direction, releasing the quarters and the deities if that ritual is part of your tradition. Close the circle and celebrate safely.

After the ceremony, make certain all is cleaned and cleared. If you bring it in, take it out. Make certain that the broom the couple jump goes home with them. It is a nice gesture. The broom is one of the symbols of their love, and that symbol should have a prominent place in their house for as long as they are together.

SECTION 2: Properties of Woods by Species

Now, it's time to discuss in depth each wood appropriate for making brooms. The order, family, genus, and species will be listed. Other categories include whether the wood has male energy, female energy, or the energy of both; what element or elements are represented; and which god(s) or goddess(es) are sacred to the wood. Where we have experience, we will also give you an example of how to use the broom in circle (or if the broom is not suited for circle, then what to do with it) and how to take care of it.

Energy

In the 1998 movie *Practical Magic*, the aunts do a ritual to eliminate a spirit from one of the two sisters. One of the aunts directs the others to form a circle of brooms head to bristle. On a non-magical level, that's a wonderful scene because it makes everyone in the group—mostly non-magic practitioners with modern brooms—feel as though they are relevant to the ritual. However, on a magical and practical level, the scene just makes sense.

We have talked about wands and brooms being like batteries. If the broom is a battery, and let's say the head of the broom is the positive end and the bristles are negative, then to join brooms head to bristles would be to join batteries positive to negative.

You have put batteries into your remote, flashlight, or toy backward and gotten no power. This is the same with a broom. If you use the incorrect end or attempt to join two or more brooms head to head or bristles to bristles, then you are negating the energy of the broom. And if you do that, your ritual, spell, or working will fail and you may not understand why.

So let us offer the rule of thumb for brooms again: Think of your broom as a battery. It will work so much better if you remember that energy flows through the broom in either direction but must then, when used in tandem with other brooms, flow into receptive ends.

Positive or Negative?

Energy isn't just positive and negative in the sense of electricity. Energy is also positive and less than positive. We hesitate to say *negative* because that gives a connotation of evil. But we might go as far as to say *light energy* and *dark energy*. *Light energy* is the energy used for good, for healing, for protection of oneself and one's loved ones, etc. *Dark energy* is the antithesis of positive energy. It is the aggressive, confrontational, and first-strike energy used to harm, curse, or damage a target. It is important to remember that magic is not just for the good.

Witches need to be aware that not only is magic preventative and preemptive, but it is also retributive. We caution anyone to think very long and hard before you embark on a path of dark magic, either offensive or defensive. Baneful magic is not something to be taken lightly. Any aggression against another will come back on you threefold. If after careful thought, you still wish to proceed, then go ahead. Remember, however, oftentimes the spell won't work the way you think it will. Be careful.

So how do we look at where woods fall in respect to energy? We have found that a scale of positive to dark with a neutral point in the middle is the best way to approach this. Below is that scale from holly, the most positive-energy wood there is, to poison ivy, the darkest. There is no perfectly positive or negative wood. Every dark-energy wood has a little positive in it or it wouldn't grow, and every positive-energy wood has a little negative in it or it wouldn't die.

Vibration Rankings

Everything vibrates with a specific energy. Wood is no different. With use, you will realize that the energy is not observable but rather evident in a metaphysical way. Those who have never felt the energy of a wand or a new athame won't understand this, but in time, everyone can experience the energy of their tools. It just takes being open to it.

Below is a ranking of where each wood falls on the scale of energy from most positive to most negative. Vibrational energy is relative to the positive or less-than-positive energy of the wood. Think of it as an attitude. Many woods are positive in nature. They will do little or no harm in their use. However, other woods are purely dark in their usage, as in the case of poison ivy, and should be treated as such. This ranking is open to interpretation though. And on any given day, any of these woods may shift depending on how "they" feel about what they are being asked to do or how they are being treated. Here is the ranking list:

Ranking	Wood
99	Holly
98	Willow
97	Rowan
96	Ash
95	Rosemary
94	Yew

Ranking	Wood
93	Osage orange
91	Witch hazel
90	Hornbeam
84	Apple
83	Orange
82	Cherry
82	Pear
82	Peach
82	Pecan
82	Plum (purple leaf)
81	Ginkgo
80	Persimmon
79	Magnolia
77	Golden rain tree
76	Olive
75	Dogwood
74	Mulberry
73	Elder
72	Hickory (shagbark)
70	Maple
69	Adler
68	Laurel
67	Eastern red cedar
66	Douglas fir
66	Spruce
65	Sycamore
61	Elm

Ranking	Wood
60	Black locust
59	Wisteria
58	Beech
57	Birch (river or white)
56	Chestnut
55	Oak
54	Hemlock
53	Hawthorn
53	Deodar cedar
52	Sumac
51	Pine
50	Poplar
49	Tulip tree
45	Fig
33	Hackberry
32	Privet
31	Cottonwood
30	Sweet gum
24	Crepe myrtle
20	Mimosa
12	Supplejack
10	Black walnut
8	Datura
6	Ebony
5	Padauk (African variety)
1	Poison ivy

The neutral poplar is not in the center of the chart above. That is because there are more positive-energy woods than dark ones. And even some of the woods below poplar are not necessarily dark; they are just not as positive as those above the center point. Woods like privet and sweet gum have very beneficial properties. They just have attitudes that make them problematic to work with at times.

In this section, we will detail specifics about many different woods. These wood selections will get you started on your broom-making magical journey. Every listing will show the wood's associated deities, elements, and other properties. We have also noted how to work with the wood in your broom crafting and suggested uses for spells and rituals within the magical circle.

Finally, we want to offer a warning: Some of these woods are toxic. Others, depending on whether you are allergic or not, are detrimental to your health. All proper care should be used when working with those woods. We will mention what woods are most dangerous, but any wood may be of issue if you have an allergy to that specific wood.

This list is alphabetical to make it easier to find the wood.

Alder

Order: Fagales
Family: Betulaceae
Genus: *Alnus*
Species: *rubra*
Energy: Feminine
Frequency: 69
Elements: Air, water, and fire
God: Bran
Goddess: Freya
Property: Water protection

Alder is as much a northern tree as magnolia is a southern one. The alder is prolific in northern North America in what would be considered the temperate zones. It is found in wet ground around swamps and low-standing water.

Because of its growing habits, alder trees make an excellent broom for elemental water magic. You can also use this broom for protection against water damage, high water, or flooding.

In the Magical Circle: Home Protection

In a magical circle, you can take your alder broom to the western quarter point. Hold the broom in both hands and begin to sweep counterclockwise. As you sweep, concentrate on forming a protective circle around you, your property, and your family from the rains that bring the floods and deep waters. Once back at the western quarter, thank the broom for its assistance. Place the broom on your altar until the end of the ritual.

Working with Alder

Alder, like many of the deciduous woods, needs to be worked green or freshly cut. You will get the best results. If you wait until the wood dries, which usually happens at the six- or eight-week mark, it will fight you until you either give up or get lucky and finish the project.

Apple

Order: Rosales
Family: Rosaceae
Genus: *Malus*
Species: *domestica*
Energy: Feminine
Frequency: 84
Elements: Air, water
God: Zeus
Goddess: Diana
Properties: Love, passion, deception

The apple is one of those trees that is found all over North America. There are even apple varieties that prosper in Florida and other hot climates where fruits such as apple don't thrive. As a landscape architecture student, Gypsey found it hilarious that the apple and the rose were of the same family, Rosaceae, because one is always referred to as a tree (apple), and one is always referred to as a bush (rose), when in reality both could be technically called either.

Apple is the first of the fruit trees listed in this section. Even though each fruit has different characteristics, the general description of their uses and properties are the same. The apple is a tree of love or deception depending on whether you believe the myths about Adam, Eve, the serpent, and the apple.

In the Magical Circle: Love or Not

The apple is a good wood for magic done in correspondence with the cardinal direction south. The apple itself is a hot-blooded fruit. It exudes love and passion, and yes, a little deception from time to time, so be careful when using it magically.

Whisk brooms are especially useful in apple since the small sweeping motion emulates the motions of two lovers. When using the apple broom, try to speak of love and passion only. Avoid discussing deception. Love cannot survive with deception present, and even though this broom is capable of both, it would rather be a lover than a liar.

Apple rituals are ones of love and passion. They exude these traits and are anxious to help in either finding or assisting with love. If you are in need of a little obfuscation, then apple is a good wood to use. It will respond well to your needs and allow you to cloud your actions or convey that which is not accurate or true to others. Be wary, though, of these actions. Consequences abound when using woods for purposes that are less than fair and equitable.

In a ritual circle, begin with cleaning the circle with your broom from the west if you are trying to hide something. Sweep outward in a counterclockwise direction. When the ritual is completed, repeat the procedure again from the west and again counterclockwise and always sweeping outward.

If the ritual is for love, then begin in the east, move in a clockwise direction, and sweep inward. Once the circle is cleaned, then preform your ritual and, upon closing, repeat the process from the east, moving clockwise and sweeping in.

A good note to remember on this is love in, hide out. Which means that if you are working with love, you want the energy coming in. If you are trying to hide something, you want the energy going out.

Working with Apple

We love working with apple. The fragrance that fills the shop when the bark is peeled or ground off and as the wood is worked is heavenly. The wood may have a pink hue to it depending on the species of apple or the age of the tree. The coloration will fade with time in some cases, but in others, the pink remains in the wood, and when sealed, is there for the duration of the broom.

Ash

Order: Lamiales
Family: Oleaceae
Genus: *Fraxinus*
Species: *americana*
Energy: Masculine
Frequency: 96
Elements: All four, works well with all elements
God: Odin
Goddesses: Frigg, Minerva
Properties: Weather magic, strength, prosperity

Ash is one of the most prolific woods there is and thrives in many parts of the world with the exception of Antarctica and portions of South America. The tree is usually referred to as either *ash* or *white ash*.

In the Magical Circle: Electrical Magic

Magically, the ash is very good for working with electricity and therefore should be considered when doing weather magic or magic containing lightning. Care should always be used when dealing with electricity, and electrical storms are highly unpredictable, so take extreme caution.

Whether you are trying to cause weather or trying to abate the storm, the ash will respond well and give you good results. Remember, though, that if you are conducting ritual in an actual lightning storm, then the broom will do little to protect you from a lightning strike. Therefore, exercise caution when working with anything electrical.

When opening a ritual or circle with the ash broom during a storm, always start at east, where all things begin, and, holding the broom with the bristles-end outward, walk clockwise around the circle. Ask the storm to bring you energy safely and to channel it into whatever project or use you are asking for. Once back at your starting point, place the broom on the altar and continue your ritual.

In closing the circle, start at east again but go counterclockwise with the handle end pointing outward. Thank the storm for its presence and ask the storm to keep the rest of its energy for future use. Once back at east, you may disperse the circle.

Working with Ash

Ash is a hardwood but not as hard as hornbeam, black locust, or crepe myrtle. The wood is clean, and turning ash is easy if done green rather than dry. Sanding is best done with power tools, especially if the wood is allowed to dry out. Then again, that's the way with many of these woods.

Beech

Order: Fagales
Family: Fagaceae
Genus: *Fagus*
Species: *sylvatica*
Energy: Feminine
Frequency: 58
Elements: Fire, water
Gods: Odin, Zeus
Goddesses: Hel, Ceridwen
Properties: Growing and harvesting, health, ridding of pests and negativity

The beech tree is found throughout North America and is one of the more prolific trees in the northern states. It is identifiable by its smooth gray bark and its leaves, which are slightly rounded, deep green, and with points at the leaf edges.

In the Magical Circle: Cleansing

Magically, beech is a solid wood for anything related to the element of earth or for anything related to our planet. For example, growing and harvesting rituals are most successful when using a beech broom. The beech broom will sweep away pests, negative energies, and ill thoughts while sweeping in health, bountifulness, and great agricultural success.

After the circle has been called and opened, take your beech broom, go to the western quarter, and begin to sweep outward. It doesn't matter which way you walk; the results will be the same. As you sweep outward, say or think of the pests, negativity, or aggression that you wish to eliminate in your life. Once you are back to the western quarter, walk the entire circle again, but this time sweep inward, either saying or concentrating on collecting positive energies. When you are done, close your circle as you normally would.

Working with Beech

Beech is very easy to work. It is soft and clean (or clear), meaning there are few knots or dark areas caused by insects or disease. But because it is so easy to work, you may stop paying attention and gouge the broom handle. Take your time, or the plane or chisel can slip through the wood. However, that's something you should be aware of while working with any of these woods, not just beech.

Birch

Order: Fagales
Family: Betulaceae
Genus: *Betula*
Species: *nigra* (river), *papyrifera* (white)
Energy: Feminine
Frequency: 57
Element: Water
God: Thor
Goddess: Freya
Properties: Winter solstice, water rituals

Birch is a prolific and persistent tree in most states along the Eastern Seaboard from Maine to Florida. It is found along most riverbeds, lakes, swamp fringes, and wherever there is standing water. Like the willow, birch is often planted for water control, although it's not as good as the willow or the cypress. Be careful when harvesting birch limbs from living trees. The limbs are very brittle, and they have a tendency to fall easily. The river birch is known for widow-makers, the loose limbs that fall off and kill loggers or other unsuspecting passersby.

In the Magical Circle: Prosperity

Birch is the wood for rituals corresponding with the element of water. You can use your birch broom for the winter solstice when you are requesting a bountiful and profitable new year.

When using a birch broom in circle, always begin and end in the west. Open your circle with your birch broom in the reverse position (i.e., the handle pointing down like a plow blade would turn the earth) and walking clockwise. Continue to hold it as such while walking clockwise around the circle, making a motion with the broom as if shoveling or plowing. When completed, place the broom on the altar and place some good growing soil next to it. When the ritual is completed, take the broom and close the circle from east and walk counterclockwise. Once the circle is closed, take the soil to your garden or field and spread it.

Working with Birch

Chelsea loves working with river birch because the grain is amazing and the patterns when polished or sealed come through with a darkness that off-sets the light wood to project an almost artistic canvas look. Work the wood green if you wish to remove a lot of wood from the limb. However, if the limb is well fashioned to be a broom handle already, then let it dry and work it with a hand sander or by hand with a wood plane or sandpaper.

Black Locust

Order: Fabales
Family: Fabaceae
Genus: *Robinia*
Species: *pseudoacacia*
Energy: Feminine
Frequency: 60
Elements: Earth, water
God: Amaethon
Goddesses: Ceridwen, Hecate, the Morrigan
Property: Binding or unbinding the will of others

Black locust is found throughout the Appalachian area of the United States, and there is also a band of the trees along the Oklahoma-Arkansas border. The trees are shade trees and have attractive white flowers when in bloom. There is a use for the tree that is beneficial other than shade and wood: the flowers are a honeybee heaven. The honey from the black locust is famous throughout the world. For this reason alone, the tree is important to prevent the collapse of hives across the country.

In the Magical Circle: Binding and Unbinding

A broom of black locust will be on par with hornbeam. It is strong, will protect the user and those in circle, and will assist in either binding the wills of others to you or unbinding them from you. To protect yourself from such binding, cast the circle with your broom starting from the south, the quarter of fire and destruction. While casting clockwise, state that you will not be bound to the will of whoever is against you. Once back at south, place the broom on the altar and continue your circle. In closing, again take the broom at south and, going counterclockwise, state as you walk, "I send back anything that binds and ties me to [the name of the individual you feel is binding or tying you]." This should take care of any issues you are having or will have with that individual.

Working with Black Locust

Both of us love black locust. As a woodworker, Gypsey made mallets of black locust for other woodworkers. Turning this wood green is a joy, and it moves quickly and evenly on her lathe. Chelsea turns green black locust into bowls that, once dry, will outlast any other wooden bowl. It has a decorative grain, which we believe is why many furniture and wood manufacturers use it. Further, it's a trash tree, meaning it grows quickly, is aggressive and invasive, and will push out other species. For this reason, it's harvested heavily in some areas for the above uses.

We've said this about almost every wood: work it green. However, for this wood it is essential. Similar to hemlock, if you allow the wood to season, you will probably never get it to do what you want it to. We've both let some of our black locust sit too long and it ended up on the bonfire pile because there was nothing either of us could do to it. You have been warned.

Black Walnut

Order: Fagales
Family: Juglandaceae
Genus: *Juglans*
Species: *nigra*
Energy: Masculine
Frequency: 10
Elements: Air, fire
Gods: Thor, Vishnu, Zeus
Goddesses: Aphrodite, Artemis, Astarte, Diana, Hel
Property: Protection

Black walnut is the protecting father of the tree world. The juglone oil drips off the twigs and leaves, killing anything under its canopy but its own. This allelopathic behavior should be remembered if you plant anything downhill of the tree. Rain will spread the oil in a larger perimeter than the tree canopy.

In the Magical Circle: Protection

This wood makes excellent protective brooms. A black walnut broom above the door or by the jamb will protect those in the house and return evil back to those projecting it.

In a circle, use the broom to cast from north, the quarter of stability and strength, and cast clockwise. Whatever you need protection from, ask the circle and specifically the broom to grant it. The broom will do the rest.

Working with Black Walnut

Gypsey absolutely loves black walnut. The wood is dark, well grained, and easy to work. It also darkens and gets much harder with age. Further, the energy of the black walnut is exceptional. The juglone oil that courses through the tree forms an energy that continues long after the piece is cut and worked.

Cedar, Deodar

Order: Pinales
Family: Pinaceae
Genus: *Cedrus*
Species: *deodara*
Energy: Masculine
Frequency: 53
Elements: All
Gods: Osiris, Ra
Goddesses: Lakshmi, Shiva, Sita
Property: Healing

Deodar cedar is one of the true cedars. The name comes from the two Sanskrit words that translate to the "wood of the God."[29] The tree is native to Central Asia; however, it has been used as a specimen plant for over one hundred years in the United States and may be found in almost all states. The campus of Clemson University in South Carolina provides a good example of how deodar cedar has acclimated to the states. The trees were planted over one hundred years ago and today are 40–60 feet high.

In the Magical Circle: Healing

Magically speaking, deodar cedar is a direct link to your gods. Also keep in mind that the deodar cedar broom is exceptionally needy. The wood wants to be the center of attention. Deodar cedar will often be difficult to control if put in a circle with another wood other than white willow. Consider what other wooden tools you have, whether it's a wand, an athame handle, or even decorations on the altar, before using a deodar cedar broom.

29. Alfred C. Andrews, "Acclimatization of Citrus Fruits in the Mediterranean Region," *Agricultural History* 35, no. 1 (1961): 35–46, https://www.jstor.org/stable/3740992.

If you wish to use a deodar broom in a healing circle, we recommend you do it in tandem with a white willow broom. The cedar will cause a direct link to your deity, and the willow broom will bring the needed healing to the situation. These two in tandem will give you the best result for what you are attempting. Start the deodar broom at the north quarter and the willow broom at south. As you pass each other at east and west, tap the brooms three times together and ask out loud for the powers to join for the healing or health of whomever. Once you are back to your originating quarter, take both brooms to the altar and lay them next to each other with the bristles touching. After the circle is closed, return them to where they came from. Make certain to thank them for their participation in your ritual.

Working with Deodar Cedar

Deodar cedar is a clear wood to work with when younger, but older trees might have small knots where the branches were. The wood is soft and the smell is pleasant when working in a confined space. As with all cedars, the wood not only makes a good broom from the larger branches but may be worked in planks to form your magical storage box.

Cedar, Eastern Red

Order: Pinales
Family: Cupressaceae
Genus: *Juniperus*
Species: *virginiana*
Energy: Masculine
Frequency: 67
Elements: Earth, fire
Gods: Loki, Tyr, Baldur
Goddesses: Hel, the Morrigan
Properties: Money, business

The eastern red cedar is not actually a cedar even though it's called one. It's a member of the juniper genus. The red spans the entire United States, and in the Texas Hill Country, the pollen is detrimental at some times of the year to those with respiratory issues.

In the Magical Circle: Money

Red cedar is very good for spells and rituals involving money and business.

If you wish to open your circle with the red cedar, do that from the north. Take your broom and sweep inward from the north quarter and think of prosperity coming your way. Do not ask for money specifically. You may be better off with some other form of wealth, and the broom will know what you need. Once the circle is open, take a small glass of gin and sprinkle it on each quarter. Ask the gods to partake with you. If you don't drink, then put the glass to your nose and breathe in deeply. Feel the energy of the liquid. Once you close the circle, repeating what you did at opening, pour the rest of the gin into the firepit and thank the gods for their assistance. Be cautious since the alcohol in the gin may cause the fire to flare.

Working with Eastern Red Cedar

While deodar cedar wood is white, the eastern red cedar is, well, as its name implies, red. If given the choice, both Gypsey and Chelsea will take an eastern red cedar over a deodar cedar any day. The color of the cedar is amazing, and the smell fills the room. Eastern red cedar is brittle. It splinters and cracks easily, and if you are trying to work it down to a finer dimension such as a wand or a thin-handled dusting broom, then your chances of success are greatly reduced. The eastern red cedar gouges very easily, which would be expected by the utter softness of the wood. Therefore, caution is warranted when working on this wood, especially if you have a limited amount of good pieces.

Cherry

Order: Rosales
Family: Rosaceae
Genus: *Prunus*
Species: spp.
Energy: Feminine
Frequency: 82
Elements: Fire, water
Gods: Thor, Mars
Goddesses: Artemis, the Morrigan
Properties: Desire, handfasting, immortality

All cherry trees fall into this category, not just the popular ones found here in the United States. This information includes the many different cherry trees throughout the world and, to be clear, not all of them are fruiting. Cherry trees are an iconic symbol in Japan, where their blossoms are a national treasure and tourist attraction.

In the Magical Circle: Manifesting Intent and Desire

Cherry brooms are the best brooms to jump during handfasting rituals. Magically, the wood is strong with love and desire. If you want to be happy and prosperous in love or relationships, then place a cherry broom above or by the inside of your front door. Cherry wood has been said to promote long life, leading to immortality, but we've never met anyone immortal so that is a rumor.

A cherry broom is best used during the dark moon. The absence of light gives it extra strength and power. Whatever you are casting the circle for will have a better chance to succeed. Place the cherry broom on your altar. Use a cherry broom to open and close the circle as your tradition dictates. Once the circle is open, take the cherry broom and, from east, where all things begin, sweep inward, walking in a clockwise direction. Ask the broom to facilitate your desires in a safe and beneficial manner.

Working with Cherry

Cherry is a brittle wood when dry but relatively easy to work when green. The branches that make up your brooms will be crooked because it's hard to find a straight-enough piece of cherry wood to make a broom that looks like the traditional broom of yore. However, it's that uniqueness and the color of the wood that makes cherry so sought after for brooms. As the wood ages, it takes on a deeper and deeper color to make the broom stand out at any circle or abode. You may either debark the broom or leave the bark in situ since the color of the bark is also an attractive attribute to the broom.

Chestnut

Order: Fagales

Family: Fagaceae

Genus: *Castanea*

Species: *dentata*

Energy: Masculine

Frequency: 56

Elements: Fire, air, water

God: Zeus

Goddesses: Artemis, Diana

Properties: Divination, spiritual cleansing

This tree is prevalent in the US, and it also appears in various translations of the Bible. In the Old Testament, it's mentioned in Genesis 30:37 and Ezekiel 31:8. However, what these verses are actually talking about is most likely the "plane tree": *Platanus orientalis*.[30] It is also a fixture in American literature—the most famous being Henry Wadsworth Longfellow's poem "The Village Blacksmith," where the line is "Under a spreading chestnut-tree."[31]

The chestnut is found throughout the northern states, predominantly in New England, westward as far as Ohio, and into some of the norther sections of the southern states. The nut has been important as a food source for both human and animal, and flour ground from the dried nuts were a staple in previous generations.

30. "Chestnut-tree," McClintock and Strong Biblical Cyclopedia, accessed February 11, 2025, https://www.biblicalcyclopedia.com/C/chestnut-tree.html.
31. Henry Wadsworth Longfellow, "The Village Blacksmith," Poets.org, accessed December 2, 2024, https://poets.org/poem/village-blacksmith.

In the Magical Circle: Psychic Cleansing

The chestnut tree is a symbol of intelligence and may inspire divination and spiritual travel when used properly. This is also an excellent broom for clearing out your psychic trash.

The cardinal direction east is the best place to use the chestnut broom when in circle. Work your magic as the sun is rising. As you sweep outward, in either direction, dismiss all your visionary issues and your psychic and magical trash, sending it all back from where it came. Once done with the circle, close it, thanking the guardians of the east for their patience and guidance in assisting you.

Working with Chestnut

Chestnut wood has some amazing grains. Take that into consideration when making your broom handle, for those grains will make your piece beautiful. If you decide not to lacquer the broom, then a light coat of butcher block oil is enough to bring out the grain. Anything too heavy may take longer to dry and be sticky if you wish to use the broom quickly after completion.

Cottonwood

Order: Malpighiales
Family: Salicaceae
Genus: *Populus*
Species: spp.
Energy: Masculine
Frequency: 31
Elements: Water, air
God: Tyr
Goddess: Hecate
Properties: Dark energy, aggression, protection

Cottonwood was heavily planted in many areas of the United States due to its fast growth and easy maintenance. However, those folks planting groves failed to realize that the root structures are too weak to support the weight of a fully grown tree. Therefore, the trees eventually outgrew their foundation and fell over—often.[32] The cottonwood tree has a number of species that span the entire United States. This issue with poor root stability is not exclusive to one area of the country. Adding to that problem, the "feathers" of the seed tails are hazardous to those with breathing issues and anyone with a home heating system with a filter. The cottonwood spirals clog up the filters like they clog up the lungs of those around them, causing severe damage due to overheating of filtration systems.

In the Magical Circle: Baneful Work

Keeping the previous facts in mind, this wood is wonderful for baneful magic. This is one of the few times we are talking about taking the offense,

32. Georgia Muenzler, lecture, master's program of landscape architecture, University of Oklahoma, 1989.

but it won't be the only. Remember, magic works both ways: light and dark. And at times, it can be very dark.

When using a cottonwood broom, it is best to commence your ritual circle in the dead of night, and, if possible, during the darkest of the new moon. The tree likes the dark and will give you your best results then. When opening, running, and closing circle, use the least amount of light possible that you can safely see with. Place the broom on the altar. Then, start your circle at north. If you are able to find a cottonwood wand, or, better yet, make one from the cast off of the broom handle you are making, build the circle with that.

Once the circle is cast, take the broom from the altar and, facing south, hold the broom above your head. Slowly point the positive end of the broom, the handle end, toward whatever you are protecting or aggressing against. If you are not certain where the aggression is coming from, then turn in a complete circle with your broom extended outward. State your intentions to protect yourself and your loved ones or properties from damage or aggression from the outside. Or if you are casting against someone, then state the reason for the aggression and who or what you are dealing with. When completed, place the broom back on the altar and close the circle.

Working with Cottonwood

Cottonwood is not a hard wood to work with. It is generally soft, and even if you get the branches dry, they will work well with either sharp hand or power tools. As with using the broom, we recommend you create the broom during the dark and new moons. If you choose to work in the light of your shop during the noonday hour, you will still get a good-looking broom and it will work to sweep the floors and your front porch. But just don't expect it to do much else. This wood loves the dark, and even though you will need light in your shop to work the wood, it's the time of night and the time of month that will stimulate the energies for the broom to do its best magic.

Crepe Myrtle

Order: Myrtales
Family: Lythraceae
Genus: *Lagerstroemia*
Species: *indica*
Energy: Masculine
Frequency: 24
Element: Air
God: Rudra
Goddesses: Artemis, Hathor, Aphrodite, Astarte
Property: Escape

Crepe myrtle is found at most big-box greenhouses and nurseries. Where the weather hits freezing, the tree is oftentimes the size of a shrub and is cut back at about 5 feet each year to maintain it as such. In the Deep South, including Florida and the Gulf Coast states, the trees may grow over 20 feet tall. Gypsey has about a dozen of these at her farm, and in the spring and early summer, they fill the air with a sweet scent and the scenery with pink, red, and white flowers.

In the Magical Circle: Finding Safety

The wood makes a great escape broom. While flying on a broom is a metaphor, escape is not. From time to time, we all want or need to escape, whether it's a bad situation, the pressures of day-to-day life, or something more nefarious. The Japanese refer to this wood as *Monkey Slip* due to the slick nature of the bark. This is what you want in an escape broom.

Use it to sweep yourself away. Once the circle is open, sweep in a counterclockwise direction from north. As you sweep, envision what you are escaping from and that you will be prepared to leave whatever is holding or threatening your safely. Once the circle has been cleansed, take clean water and sprinkle the water on the broom to wash away all the negativity. If necessary, you may repeat this ritual as needed.

Working with Crepe Myrtle

Few woods are as hard as crepe myrtle green or dry. The wood has an odd gray color when dry that gives it a pretty hue that is hard to match in the field. Working with crepe myrtle, though, is difficult due to its hardness. Make certain your tools are very sharp and wear heavy gloves. More than once, we have both slipped with a chisel and would have seriously done damage to ourselves had it not been for heavy gloves. When you are ready to finish the wood, wait for it to dry some. The wood takes sealer well but not when wet. The wood seems to just ignore the sealant, and it wells up on the wood in droplets, which may be annoying if you are in a hurry. Don't be in a hurry.

Datura

Order: Solanales
Family: Solanaceae
Genus: *Datura*
Species: spp.
Energy: Feminine
Frequency: 8
Element: Air
Gods: Erebus, Hypnos, Indra,
Goddesses: Nyx, Hecate, Selene, Nott, Hel, Kali
Property: Cleansing of negativity
Warning: Poisonous

Datura will kill you. Make no mistake about that. It is a powerful plant with a poisonous attitude. The leaves emit an oil that can cause serious inflammation to the skin. The seeds, if taken internally, can be fatal if consumed in large enough dosages.

The datura plant grows to heights of over 6 feet and the stalks, while flimsy as a fresh plant, will harden when dried. The plant is often sold with the name *moon flower* because it blooms at night. Bees love the flowers, and if you have large amounts of them on your property, then the entire section of the garden will vibrate from the bees. But remember what we started the first paragraph with: Datura will kill you.

In the Magical Circle: Protection

Datura makes an excellent broom for protection. Magically, it is on the far end of the dark-energy spectrum and is not a broom to be used lightly. When casting or cleaning with a datura broom, make certain you are free of the encumbrances of negative thoughts or actions. Clear your mind of anything other than the task at hand. The broom will pick up on anything out of place and will react to those thoughts exactly as you are thinking them. And the energy from this broom is formidable. Be careful with its use. You have been warned.

Similar to the other darker-energy woods such as poison ivy and padauk, datura will protect you. If you need such protection, wait till a new moon. Cast your circle from south, where the fire energy is strongest. Using your broom, sweep outward in a clockwise direction while asking the datura broom to cast away any dangers that may exist and to create a ring of safety around you and yours. When the sweeping is completed, place the datura broom back on the south-quarter altar until the completion of the ritual. Before you close the circle, repeat the procedure, again sweeping outward in a clockwise direction and requesting safety for you and yours.

Working with Datura

Datura will fool you with its softness when fresh, but dried, it makes for a very strong yet lightweight broom handle. If you weave the vines like macramé before drying the stalks, when dry, the wound or woven vines will produce a solid and rather attractive handle for your long or short broom. You may want to wear gloves and a mask due to the nature of the plant, and vines are easier to cut wet than dry. So if you plan on making a wrapped handle from these vines, cut, then wrap, then tie off at both ends with some twine to keep them from unraveling.

Datura stems must then be dried thoroughly before any further use. They are easily cut and only require light sanding to make them comfortable to hold. Finish with a light coat of polyurethane to keep the stems protected and from reabsorbing moisture. As said above, you should use protective gloves and a mask when working with datura. Once you are finished, the wood is safe to handle.

Treat the wood with respect and don't take chances. If you are not comfortable working with a plant that is possibly dangerous, then we strongly recommend that you don't. However, you may use this broom as any other once the wood has dried and been treated.

Dogwood

Order: Cornales
Family: Cornaceae
Genus: *Cornus*
Species: *sericea*
Energy: Masculine
Frequency: 75
Element: Fire
Gods: Cronus, Saturn
Goddess: Gaia
Properties: Ancestral magic, Southern root magic

The dogwood is an ancient tree. It is mentioned in Chaucer as a "whipple-tree."[33]

Dogwood is often thought of when one discusses the South, specifically the "Old South" due to its prominence in the southern states. It is one of two trees that are associated with Southern magic.

In the Magical Circle: Ancestral Connection

Dogwood is excellent for heritage or ancestry magic. It offers clear and concise direction and interpretation when dealing with the long dead. Dogwood is exceptional for performing a divination ritual as explained in chapter 7. You will be better served that way.

When dealing with ancestral magic, the closer to your ancestors the better. Oftentimes, that means conducting your circle in cemeteries, sometimes

33. Geoffrey Chaucer, *The Canterbury Tales,* trans. and ed. Nevill Coghill, Penguin Classics (Penguin Books, 2003), 81; Walter William Skeat, "Wipple-Tree, Otherwise Whipultre: Gaytre," in *A Student's Pastime: Being a Select Series of Articles Reprinted from "Notes and Queries,"* (Clarendon Press, 1896), 252.

late at night or when you are left to your own devices. You don't have to cast a circle. You don't even need anyone else. With your dogwood broom, carefully sweep the grave. Talk to your ancestor as you sweep. Most likely there will be grass there but oftentimes also leaves and debris. Clear what you can.

Sit facing the headstone if there is one. If not, then sit facing west. With the dogwood broom on your lap, talk to your ancestor. Ask what you need to know and be open to what you may understand in your mind. Once concluded, thank your ancestor. Before leaving, water the grass on the grave with fresh rainwater.

Working with Dogwood

Dogwood is a rather soft wood when green. And it stays relatively soft after drying. The clear, light color of the wood is attractive for brooms, and when you work with it, as with many others, you may work with it either green or dry. Gypsey personally likes working dogwood dry. It's easier to sand, and the tools will clean up any stems or knots more easily without getting bogged down in green pulp. If you clamp the broom handle onto your workbench or a sawhorse, you will quickly clean up the wood.

Douglas Fir

Order: Pinales
Family: Pinaceae
Genus: *Pseudotsuga*
Species: *menziesii*
Energy: Masculine
Frequency: 66
Elements: Air
Gods: Bacchus, Pan, Osiris
Goddesses: Artemis, Diana, Isis
Properties: Safety, security

The plight of the Douglas fir, which is the most common of the firs, is that it is not a fir at all. David Douglas named it a fir when classifying it in the later nineteenth century and no one changed it once they found the error. So, the poor Douglas fir, which is the one you will most likely find in the wilds of America, may be treated as its own tree in many respects.

In the Magical Circle: Safety and Security

Any broom made with Douglas fir will give you great amounts of safety and security, magically speaking. You may rest assured that the broom will do its best, and it's rather good at keeping things in place. However, you should also assist the broom by putting things away, keeping things orderly, and remembering, if you can, where you put them.

In circle, begin with your broom in the north. Sweep or cast clockwise and do it more slowly than you would normally. Take deep breaths and exhale fully as you sweep. Request assistance in whatever you need at each quarter, offering the broom as a go-between or liaison. Your success will be greatly enhanced if you do these simple things.

Working with the Douglas Fir

The wood of the Douglas is good to work, but the pores are open, and you will have to eventually seal the wood after sanding if you want a broom handle that will last. However, the upside is that the wood is clear and takes sealant well. The grain and fine coloration, though rather pale in comparison to the eastern red cedar, is attractive to some but kind of boring to others. To each their own.

Even if Douglas was a true fir, it would still be easy to work. Coniferous softwoods are famously forgiving in the shop, although you shouldn't be. Keep your tools sharp and your resolve true and you will have a beautiful and useful magical instrument for years.

Ebony

Order: Ericales
Family: Ebenaceae
Genus: *Diospyros*
Species: *ebenum*
Energies: Masculine and feminine
Frequency: 6
Elements: Earth, fire
God: Obatala
Goddess: Yamaya
Property: New moon

Gabon ebony is endangered due to overcutting for furniture and should not be sourced unless by authorized harvesters for propagation purposes. Most ebony that is locally available to anyone in the United States through specialty wood stores is Ceylon ebony, which is *Diospyros ebenum*.

In the Magical Circle: New Moon Magic

Ebony is on the lower level of the energy scale but doesn't have some of the baggage of poison ivy. Although it is a dark wood, not just in color but also in the energy it projects, ebony is good for defense and protection. Ebony will work with light-energy magic as well as with dark-energy magic, although it gravitates to the darker side of the pond.

However, one word of caution for ebony: Magically speaking, treat this wood as you would poison ivy or padauk. It is not as aggressive in its approach to the darker energies, but it can become so if crossed or angered. While woods like poplar are like warm puppies doing whatever you ask them to do (although not always doing it well), ebony will do what you ask but not always the way you expect it. Treat the wood with respect.

This wood is great for dark moon or new moon rituals. Use the short broom or the whisk and forgo using an actual wand. While in circle, cast and call with the whisk to sweep the energies out of the circle as one would with a larger broom. But with the ebony whisk, you are eliminating all the lighter energies and keeping the darker ones. If you are working dark energy at a new moon ritual, then you aren't too worried about lighter or even neutral energies. You are manipulating all the darker ones. Conduct your ritual. When it is completed and before you close your ritual and release your quarters, make certain you cleanse everything. You may do this with either fresh rainwater or a sage smoke cleanse. Your tools have collected dark energies, and you don't want to bring those outside of circle.

Working with Ebony

This is another excellent whisk broom wood. The pieces you can procure at specialty wood shops are large enough to make fairly good-sized handles for small sweeping brooms or whisks. And the wood takes an amazing shine when polished, so not only does it do well for you magically but it just looks darn cool on your altar and without any type of sealant.

Ebony is both an easy and difficult wood to work with depending on your tools and disposition—and I mean yours, not the wood's. If you are working on a lathe, then make certain your chisels are sharp. Ebony will "skip" and therefore gouge and not be smooth when you are done. And if you are working with hand tools, then make sure that your tools are just as sharp and you work with a steady hand and eye. Some ebonies will be soft and thus respond easily to your attempts. However, Gypsey has worked with ebony that fought her tooth and claw. Every moment at the lathe or bench was a struggle to get the wood to respond the way she wanted it to, which isn't always the way the wood wants.

Ebony may be worked at any time of the day or night and any moon phase, which is not the case with all woods. Although you will get the best results at the dark of the moon, you may also see positive results if you work in the light of day. Gypsey has worked the wood during storms, and there isn't any difference to the "feel" of the wood or the "flow" of the energy when doing such. She thinks that ebony just works itself out as it wishes and goes on its own path. That's anthropomorphic, but ebony comes across that way at times. Remember that all woods have a "sense" of what they "want" to do versus what you want them to do.

Elder

Order: Dipsacales
Family: Adoxaceae
Genus: *Sambucus*
Species: spp.
Energy: Feminine
Frequency: 73
Elements: All four
Gods: Freyr, Vulcan
Goddesses: Gaia, Hel, Venus
Property: Work with the Fae

You're probably going to be hard pressed to find an elderberry shrub large enough to make a whisk broom handle or a wand from. They just don't grow that large anymore in most of the United States due to the tree being kept as more of a shrub now. The trees, and we hazard to call them that, are usually found not more than 10–12 feet tall and a little more than an inch or two in diameter. Gypsey had one in South Carolina that was ten years old, and it was nothing more than a thick-stemmed, overgrown shrub.

The wood, though, when you find one to work with, will give you purple-black berries that are often used in liqueurs and medicinal drinks. Probably the most famous use of the drink was the play and then the movie *Arsenic and Old Lace*, where the Brewster sisters killed their lodgers with poison mixed in elderberry wine.

In the Magical Circle: Fae Magic

Many witches have come to believe that elder is the most powerful wood in the magical world thanks partly to the Harry Potter franchise with its Elder Wand. We hate to break it to you, but it's not. It's a great wand, but it's not the most powerful or the most magical. And it's a great wood if you can find a piece large enough to make a broom from.

The positive aspect of the elder is that it's sacred to the Fae, and if you are doing work with them, then use a whisk or other small broom. Since it's difficult to get a long enough length to make a full broom handle, a whisk will work exceptionally well.

When using the elder broom in circle, start at the north and work clockwise, addressing the Fae at each quarter, such as with a piece of fresh fruit, a small glass of fresh rainwater, or something shiny they can wear. Once you are done and as you are closing the circle, leave a token of thanks to the Fae on the ground in front of each quarter. They may or may not accept it, but it's better to err on the side of caution. If you fail to leave an offering and they wanted one, then you are in for a problem.

Working with Elder

The problem with working with elder, other than that it's hard to find a large enough piece, is that the wood is very pithy and too soft to hold a tool. Leaving it to dry will only make the wood porous, and if it's not rotted by the time you get to it, will be powdered. While we don't like using liquid sealants, beeswax will work on this broom. Rub the wax into the broom, and then with a clean cloth, work the wax until it forms a coating over the broom. If you are lucky, and there is a chance you may be, then the air won't get into the wood enough to dry it out long enough for you to have a few good years with your broom.

Elm

Order: Rosales
Family: Ulmaceae
Genus: *Ulmus*
Species: *americana*
Energies: Feminine and masculine
Frequency: 61
Elements: Air, earth, water
Gods: Dionysus, Hermaphroditus, Loki, Odin
Goddesses: Ceridwen, Hel, Hermaphroditus, Gaia
Property: Duality of magic

You won't see as many elms as you or your parents once did as children. Almost every city or town in the north and some in the south had an Elm Street where the elm trees lined both sides of the thoroughfare. Now, the trees are all gone, succumbing to Dutch elm disease. Those that you see are probably a newer species of disease-resistant elms, and they are most likely much smaller than the grand elms of yesteryear.

In the Magical Circle: Beyond the Binary

This tree is one of five trees in this list that are both male and female—meaning the tree is self-pollinating. It is great for energy work when you need both sides of the god and goddess pairing. Further, this wood is best used during the sign of Gemini, the twins, when both aspects are in play.

When using this broom in circle, you need two—yes, we said two—elm brooms. Each broom is held by an individual in the north. When you begin to cast your circle, one individual goes clockwise. The other individual goes counterclockwise. It doesn't matter who does which way. Practice this so that you each stop at the quarters at the same time and pass each other at south.

While in circle you may perform whatever work you need that requires both male and female energies. Don't be afraid of one overpowering the other. The brooms will keep each other in check even if the individuals do not. The elm is that powerful when working. When you are done with the ritual, repeat the circle but the other way so that you unwind, so to speak, what you wound up earlier. After you've done it once, you'll feel the duality of the energies and look forward to performing that ritual again.

Working with Elm

Elm is a joy to work. It responds nicely to tools and will sand to an almost-perfect smoothness. Further, it's relatively easy to find a piece large enough for a full broom handle if you are able to find an elm. And that's the crux of this wood: It's rare and it knows it. And it also knows it's special. If you've never worked with a prima donna wood before, then this is it. But it's worth it in the end. Remember that.

Fig

Order: Rosales
Family: Moraceae
Genus: *Ficus*
Species: *carica*
Energy: Masculine
Frequency: 45
Element: Fire
Gods: Dionysus, Jupiter
Goddesses: Isis, Juno
Property: Eliminating shame or guilt

Fig trees are common in most areas of the United States. The most popular fig is the 'Brown Turkey' fig, and they are found in most of the big-box stores and nurseries as specimen trees that are beneficial to the owners for their fruit as well as to the wildlife for the same reason.

In the Magical Circle: Eliminating Shame and Guilt

Fig brooms are great for sweeping away shame and guilt. They are also excellent for helping to rid you of negativity that may have clung to you during your life or circumstances. It is easy to see why the writers of the Bible chose to use the fig leaf as the covering for Adam and Eve after eating the forbidden fruit. The leaves are quite large and spread out, and they can cover even the amplest of spicy bits on the body.

When using a fig broom in circle, start from either the east or the west. If you are trying to rid yourself of something, such as a nasty situation or something you did that you regret or that has caused harm to another, then begin in the west where the sun sets. Sweep with your broom clockwise, pushing all the issues you have out into the aether to be washed away with the next cleansing rain. If you are trying to protect yourself from someone else who is attempting to lay guilt on you or blame you for something you are innocent of, then start your circle in the east and sweep counterclockwise. As you sweep past each quarter, ask the guardians to protect you from your assailants and send back whatever they are casting toward you. Even though we talk about dark magic and preemptive strikes, it does none of us any good to incur the wrath of the gods by breaking the rule of do no harm. Better to ask the gods to allow the harm to be returned unaccepted to the one sending it. Let them worry about the ramifications.

Working with Fig

Fig is a lovely wood to work with. It is soft and clear with little brittleness if worked green. If you are harvesting a broom handle, then you may be coppicing a growth off the trunk. *Coppicing* is when you cut back part or all of the tree to allow fresh growth. Coppicing is usually done along fencerows and was historically a way of regenerating firewood for winter from the new growth of the year or multiple years previously. If that is the case, thank the tree for the piece and cut the piece as close to the trunk as possible. Avoid the sap, though. It is poisonous to both humans and animals. Gloves and protective gear are recommended. Remember to either paint or apply beeswax to the cut to prevent insects and other nasties from damaging the trunk and thus the entire tree.

Gingko

Order: Ginkgoales
Family: Ginkgoaceae
Genus: *Ginkgo*
Species: *biloba*
Energy: Feminine
Frequency: 81
Element: Earth
God: Wong Tai Sin
Goddess: Guanyin
Property: Aging

The gingko is a new addition (i.e., two hundred years) to the American landscape. When first planted, both male and female trees were prevalent; however, once the general population realized how putrid the smell of the female tree was, they were rightly shunned. Now, the trees that you see in parks and gardens are most likely males that were either cloned or grafted.

Unlike cottonwood, the ginkgo is ideally suited for areas where there is a greater amount of strong wind. The roots of the tree run deep, and the trunk is strong enough to withstand the winds thrown against it. Also, when fruiting, the gingko will produce a lovely nut with a slightly bitter taste that's not too off putting. Be warned, though, that the nut may be toxic if eaten in large quantities, and children should be kept from eating them to avoid disturbance of their internal systems.

In the Magical Circle: Aging

Magically, the gingko broom will assist those of a certain age with seeking guidance as they near their end. We are not saying that this is the broom to use if you are fearful of death or if you want to seek longevity in life; we're saying that this broom will assist you in accepting your place in the natural order of aging and settle your mind as to where you are and where you have yet to go. Place the broom closest to where you sleep, either on a wall or in a corner where the broom may keep in contact with you.

Ginkgo will also assist you in aging better. Some of us age easily and some age difficultly, wracked with illnesses that may hasten our aging process. We all age, and ginkgo can help.

The ginkgo broom is not for circle casting. This is a house ritual broom. Use your broom to clean your house. Sweep the floors with the broom and talk to the house as you do that. Remind the house that it is where you live and it is where you age. Ask the house to only bring in positive energies and repel the darker ones so that you may be healthy for a longer amount of time. At the same time that you are doing this, sweep each room with the broom and remind the broom that you are moving all dust and other detritus out of the house so that it does not affect you and your health.

Working with Ginkgo

Caution should be used when working with ginkgo. The oils in the bark and the sap cause a rash similar to poison ivy for those who are easily susceptible to plant-based rashes. Once dried or sealed, the broom will be rendered harmless, but in the process of creating your broom, caution should be sought over speed. Wear gloves and other protective gear. See the section on poison ivy or padauk for other recommendations.

Golden Rain Tree

Order: Sapindales
Family: Sapindaceae
Genus: *Koelreuteria*
Species: *paniculata*
Energy: Feminine
Frequency: 77
Element: Air
God: Ame-no-Koyane
Goddess: Ame-no-Uzume
Properties: Exploration and creativity

In landscape architecture, there is a term: *specimen tree*. That means the tree is singled out for its beauty or shade or bark or a dozen other reasons to be the center point of a garden or yard. The golden rain tree is that specimen. Its lantern-shaped flowers in either orange or yellow may be seen from a good distance and are always pleasing. It is tolerant of many biological zones, and as a result, in the Deep South it is often treated as a nuisance tree because it propagates quickly and forces out the natural growth.

In the Magical Circle: Exploration and Creativity

Using a golden rain tree broom is perfect for discovering unknown things. If you are a writer, then this broom is perfect to hang over your desk, in your office, or wherever you write to enhance your search for stories, truths, and inspiration.

If you wish to cast a circle for your endeavors, begin your circle in the east, where all things begin. Cast the circle clockwise. When you reach each quarter, stop. Spend at least thirty seconds in quiet contemplation of what you want to write or research and then light a white candle asking the guardian for assistance. Do this at each quarter. After the circle is completed, let the candle burn out. This will send all your wishes, hopes, and dreams to the aether, where those who guard such things as ideas, thoughts, and stories dwell.

Working with the Golden Rain Tree

Treat this wood with respect. This is not a wood to be quickly worked, sealed, bristled, and sent out the door. This is a thoughtful wood, a wood that has a lot to offer you, and you should be aware of that. The wood is not that hard to tool. It will take blade and scraper well and in return will give you a lovely broom for your use in circle, office, or both.

Hackberry

Order: Rosales
Family: Cannabaceae
Genus: *Celtis*
Species: *occidentalis*
Energy: Feminine
Frequency: 33
Elements: Fire, water
God: Kumugwe
Goddess: Ixchel
Property: Cleaning

The hackberry tree is both a boon and a bane to many homeowners, sportsmen, and animal lovers. It's a boon to those who appreciate the berries. For many animals that eat them, they are a solid form of nutrition either on the tree or when they fall. They are also eaten by humans as one would eat blackberries or black raspberries. However, those who do partake of the berries end up with a purple stain on their teeth, lips, and tongue similar to eating beets. The bane comes when the same berries are consumed by wildlife and then defecated. The feces turn whatever they touch purple, whether it's the grass, the water, or the walkways in parks and gardens. Fortunately, the berries are short lived and the tree isn't.

The tree is a strong deciduous specimen that will grow to exceptional height and width. It is excellent for timber if you choose to cut and mill it, although most find the wood brittle and unreliable for dimensional lumber. A hackberry broom is not just good for ritual or circle; it also makes a good cleaning broom.

In the Magical Circle: Cleansing

In ritual, use the hackberry broom to sweep out unwanted clutter that lingers in the ritual area. Sweep outward from the eastern quarter in a clockwise direction. As you do so, state that you are sweeping out the clutter and litter that has become evident in your circle, your life, or your path. Once done sweeping, place the broom on the altar and continue with your ritual. You and your space are both cleansed.

Working with Hackberry

Hackberry is a brittle wood. Its strength is in its roots and trunk, but once you cut it and dry it, the wood becomes just another leafy deciduous like sweetgum. Be aware of that before you spend your time and energy making a hackberry broom. Unless you are specifically looking for a hackberry broom to sweep out your house, we advise finding a better wood suited to your specific needs.

Hawthorn

Order: Rosales
Family: Rosaceae
Genus: *Crataegus*
Species: *arcana*
Energy: Masculine
Frequency: 53
Elements: Air, fire
Gods: Mars, Thor, Zeus
Goddesses: Brigid, Frigg
Property: Working with the Fae

Hawthorn is hard to find nowadays. It's a northern tree, and only in deep forests will you find a tree large enough to cull branches for brooms. That's sad because the tree is lovely to work with and a true legend in the forest. While it grows large if left alone, now you will likely find one that is no more than 15–20 feet tall and, at best, less than 1 foot in diameter.

In the Magical Circle: The Fae

The advantage of the hawthorn is that it is a tree of the Fae, and if you wish to work with them, then seek out this tree and make your broom from it.

Since each group of Fae are unique in their beliefs and traditions, it would be impertinent of us to tell you how to contact, work with, or bond with the Fae. Hawthorn, however, is one of the trees that you would be well served to use if the Fae are beings you wish to work with. How you converse with the Fae is up to you. Hawthorn will assist you.

Working with Hawthorn

The hawthorn is an easy wood to work with. This is not because it is exceptionally soft or clear or knot free but rather because it wants to be a magical instrument. It almost works itself. We are being a little facetious but not too much. The hawthorn will respond to you, and whatever you desire to do with it, you should have good fortune.

Hemlock

Order: Pinales
Family: Pinaceae
Genus: *Tsuga*
Species: spp.
Energy: Feminine
Frequency: 54
Element: Water
Gods: Alaunus, Dian Cécht
Goddess: Hecate
Properties: Building, spring cleaning

The hemlock tree is found throughout the United States in colder climates. There is little difference between the species. The tree is slow growing, dense, and long lived. The tree is less often used for dimensional lumber due to the fact that it is very hard to cut or form once dry. However, many barns and farmhouses in New England erected prior to the nineteenth century are hemlock.

In the Magical Circle: Spring Energy Cleaning

Magically, the hemlock makes a good spring cleaning broom for your house or apartment. A circle is not needed for this work. On the spring equinox, take your hemlock broom and, starting in the backmost corner of the house, sweep everything to the front door. It doesn't matter if you use the side or back door usually. You want everything to be swept to the door you use the most: dirt, dust, stale energy—whatever. After that, place the broom either over or behind that door, where it may guard against unwanted energies.

Working with Hemlock

Hemlock is a soft wood to work when it is green, but Gypsey reports that it is the strongest wood she ever built with when it is dry. When she was in New Hampshire years ago, she built a house out of hemlock. She felled the wood on her land and had it milled. As she progressed and the wood dried, her bricklayer realized that he had planned for the chimney in the house incorrectly. After several attempts to pull the nails and move some of the joists and rafters to accommodate the chimney, he gave up and put the chimney where it was built for. The nails just wouldn't come out. And the wood had only been cut six months earlier.

Work your hemlock dripping wet if you can. In the building trade, we call wood that wet *pond dried*, and it means that if you drive a nail all the way in, the indentation that is left from the hammer would fill up with water. That's how wet you need your hemlock to be, because once it's dry even a little, your chances of getting a good broom handle or other piece of magical equipment are greatly reduced.

Hickory (Shagbark)

Order: Fagales
Family: Juglandaceae
Genus: *Carya*
Species: *ovata*
Energy: Masculine
Frequency: 72
Elements: Earth, fire
God: Apollo
Goddess: Asintmah
Property: Moving lingering spirits along after death

The shagbark hickory is popular for magical use. This is because it's a prolific species that grows over most of the country but predominantly in the East and Midwest. It is a strong tree with edible nuts. Hickory has good bark and wood for cooking and smoking meats.

In the Magical Circle: Moving Spirits

Neither the hickory bark nor the wood are directly related to magic unless you are a chef or a kitchen witch, which at times may be the same. Then it's all magic, and your cookbook is your grimoire.

The benefit of using a hickory broom in circle is that it is helpful in moving spirits along after death. If one of your coven is having recurring dreams about, or contact from, a newly departed relative or friend, place that person in the middle of the circle. Beginning at north, cast your circle counterclockwise. While walking backward around the circle, sweep the energies out into the aether. Assure the departed that it's okay to leave and their friend or relative still on this plane will remember them and see them soon.

Once you are done casting the circle, give the broom to the individual in the center and have them say goodbye to their friend or relative while holding the broom. Then, from north, have them walk forward while sweeping outward, constantly talking to the friend or relative as they leave this plane to go to the next. By the time the circle is closed and the broom is back at north, the individual should no longer be contacted by the departed.

Working with Hickory

Work the wood green. Once it's dry, it's almost as hard as hemlock or black locust.

Holly

Order: Aquifoliales
Family: Aquifoliaceae
Genus: *Ilex*
Species: *aquifolium*
Energy: Masculine
Frequency: 99
Elements: Earth, air, fire
Gods: Freyr, Tyr, Saturn, Ares
Goddesses: Gaia, Danu
Properties: Healing, health, positive energy

It is important not to confuse holly the tree and holly the shrub. The shrub, or *Ilex cornuta*, is short, seldom growing larger than 8 feet with branches that are short, curved, and very soft to work. Holly the tree (*Ilex aquifolium*) can grow to 50 feet, with a strong, straight trunk and grain. This is the holly you want for brooms.

In the Magical Circle: Healing Energy

Either holly will work the same magically. A holly broom is incapable of doing harm. It's just not in it. It is sacred to the Druids, who would place the holly branches and leaves in their hair and the red berries are a pleasant natural augmentation.

If an individual is ill, you can place your holly broom under their bed. Continue to care for the individual, and they should recover completely.

Holly brooms are excellent at cleaning magical circles. In healing rituals, they sweep away all evil and negativity from the circle, leaving peace and well-being.

Working with Holly

When working with holly, you want to work during a full moon. We have found that raising a magical circle first will give the wood the added energy of the moon and the deities. It is, however, not required. But if possible, cast a circle around your work area at ten o'clock at night on the full moon and close the circle by two o'clock the next morning. That gives you four hours to work on your broom, but if you prepare your space and plan your time, that's enough to get a good start. As with other full or dark moon workings, it's okay to spread the work over more than one moon cycle.

Holly is an easy wood to work with. The tree is straight, clean grained, and white. We recommend that you don't seal the broom handle if you use holly. The wood is so beautiful in its natural state that any sealant may darken or cloud up and mar the wood.

Hornbeam

Order: Fagales
Family: Betulaceae
Genus: *Carpinus*
Species: *caroliniana*
Energy: Feminine
Frequency: 90
Element: Water
God: Sucellus
Goddess: Arduinna
Properties: Strength, durability

The American hornbeam is probably what you will find most often. Growing up in New Hampshire, Gypsey knew the wood as *ironwood* and used it to replace shovel, rake, and axe handles. The wood was wicked hard and when cured would be almost impossible to break, hence the term *ironwood*.

In the Magical Circle: Power Up Your Ritual

Hornbeam's magical property is what its name implies: It is a beast of strength and power. If you are needing that extra push to get your spell or ritual through the veil, then a broom of hornbeam is your answer.

Hornbeam is the broom you want to have in circle. You don't have to cast with it or even sweep with it. Hornbeam is strong enough that just placing it on your altar will give power to your ritual. Or lay down a protective fabric at the entrance to your circle and have everyone walk over the broom to invoke the power of the wood. This will hasten the successful conclusion of the ritual.

Working with Hornbeam

The hornbeam is very workable until it's not. That sounds counterintuitive, but there is no cutoff for when the wood becomes hard to work with. Therefore, we strongly recommend you do your rough work as soon as you cut the limb or shaft and then wait until it dries out to do your finish work, such as sanding and sealing. Even more than many other woods, hornbeam will warp as it dries. You may either set up a drying jig to lock it into a straight dry or let it find its natural shape. Remember, whenever you attempt to force a wood against its will, it will remember. We advise letting the wood do its own thing.

If you can get a large enough piece while it's still green, hornbeam makes a wonderful broom handle. It is an attractive wood, often clear but at times with streaks that give it a grainy look that takes sealer well.

Laurel

Order: Rosales
Family: Rosaceae
Genus: *Prunus*
Species: *laurocerasus*
Energy: Masculine
Frequency: 68
Elements: Air, fire
Gods: Apollo, Baldur
Goddess: Ceres
Property: Divination

Laurel is a very popular shrub and small tree in the South. The shrub may be trained to be a single-trunk tree and will get rather stately if properly pruned and cared for. The flowers are lovely, and the leaves are broadleaf evergreen.

In the Magical Circle: Divination

The laurel is excellent for divination, and a broom made from a laurel will be both beautiful with the curves and nuances of the wood and magically helpful in circle. A divination ritual is best performed alone. For our broom-based divination ritual, see the section on divination in chapter 7.

Working with Laurel

Working with laurel is relatively easy. The wood is clean, and, as with most woods, if you work with it green, then planes, chisels, and knives will move easily through the soft wood. I recommend you work the wood at a full moon if you wish to use the broom for divination. Cast a circle, then work from ten o'clock at night until two o'clock the next morning. Once the time runs out, close your circle and store the unfinished broom handle in dark cloth and in a closet out of the light. While the laurel doesn't shun the bright light, until you are done crafting the broom, it is best to avoid losing some of the full moon's energies to the light of day.

Magnolia

Order: Magnoliales
Family: Magnoliaceae
Genus: *Magnolia*
Species: *grandiflora*
Energy: Feminine
Frequency: 79
Element: Water
God: Freyr
Goddess: Jord
Properties: High Southern magic, divination, connecting with Gaia the mother goddess

The magnolia is an ancient tree and a tree representative of the old Deep South. *Magnolia grandiflora* predates the evolution of the bees and was originally pollinated by beetles. This is the tree you see in parks and around houses in the South with large limbs from a central trunk and flowers that are large and white.

There is another magnolia that is growing in popularity. The saucer magnolia, (*Magnolia* ×*soulangeana*) is a hybrid from the nineteenth century. The saucer magnolia blooms first and then leafs out later. Either magnolia will do the same thing.

Magnolia is a tree of the old-money rich, often planted around large, stately homes in the South. When one thinks of the typical Southern mansion, it's the magnolias that bring that image to life.

In the Magical Circle: High Southern Magic

With that in mind, the magnolia is a plantation high-magic tree as opposed to the root or crop magic of the dogwood. The difference is that of strata, or social standing. Magnolia will also provide a direct line to the mother goddess, Gaia. A broom of magnolia will give the wielder an exceptional ability to contact the Earth Mother.

While sky clad rituals are not as popular as they once were, this is a ritual best performed sky clad, which means without clothing. You want to be as close to the earth as possible, and clothing, even organically sourced, is still a barrier to you and your goddess. If you choose to do this sky clad, take all the safety and legal precautions first.

This ritual is different than all the others. The ritual begins at one quarter for opening and another quarter for closing. To open the circle, begin in the eastern quarter. Hold the broom with the bristles pointing downward and walk clockwise. As you walk the circle, stop at each quarter and request the mother goddess imbue your broom with energy from deep in the earth.

Conduct your ritual, and when you are concluded, begin the closing in the western quarter. Hold the broom with the bristles pointing upward. Stop at the quarters and thank the mother goddess for assisting you in your quest for whatever you are seeking. Once completed, the circle is open and the ritual is completed.

Working with Magnolia

Magnolia is a large wood if you get an old piece. When Gypsey was at Clemson, the university, in its questionable wisdom, chose to cut down hundred-year-old magnolias and build a computer building in the middle of the only green space on campus. According to Gypsey, the building was hideous and the trees were gone. However, she was able to get some pieces that were 6 inches across. These pieces were amazing to work as brooms, wands, or handles for magical edged tools, such as a boline. The wood was heavy but worked extremely well with tools.

Magnolia also has an odd grain that is hard to describe. It's darker in some trees and runs the length of the trunks or limbs, giving the striation an interesting look similar to crepe myrtle but different.

Maple

Order: Sapindales
Family: Sapindaceae
Genus: *Acer*
Species: *saccharum* (sugar), *rubrum* (red)
Energy: Masculine
Frequency: 70
Elements: Earth, air
God: Jupiter
Goddesses: Rhiannon, Venus, Athena
Property: Flight in thought and deeds

There are around 130 species of maples. Two of the most common are the sugar maple and the red maple, but all maples have the same properties and abilities. The red and sugar maples are susceptible to the ambrosia beetle, which burrows into the wood, depositing fungus along the way, thus giving the grain pattern of the wood a lovely coloring.

In the Magical Circle: Flight in Thoughts and Deeds

Maple brooms are ideal for creativity. The maple broom allows you to "take flight" both in your thoughts and deeds. The idea of your "thoughts taking flight" fits the usage of the maple broom better than any other.

Weavers and spinners may also want to hang a maple broom inside over their main door for protection and inspiration.

You don't need a circle or ritual to utilize the creative power of the maple broom. If you are an artist, writer, craftsperson, or inventor, hang a maple broom above your workspace. If you have an office, hang the broom above your door. If you have a shop, then hang the broom above your workbench.

Let the thoughts flow and you will increase your productivity when in the presence of a maple broom.

Working with Maple

If you're lucky enough to get fresh, green maple, then you are in for a treat in the shop. Maple that is freshly cut will almost work itself. The wood is clear and soft until it hardens, and then it begins to darken to the palette of dark maple furniture that we are all accustomed to. The trick is to get the wood early and work it.

The only downside to working maple green is that it will tend to split when it dries. The larger pieces will split from the middle out and give you a nasty crack down one side. The larger pieces are more prone to that, but even pieces the size of broom shafts will split and crack if not dried slowly. And even then, you have a fifty-fifty chance that the broom handle will crack.

Mimosa

Order: Fabales

Family: Fabaceae

Genus: *Mimosa*

Species: spp.

Energy: Feminine

Frequency: 20

Elements: Air, water

God: Saturn

Goddess: Artemis

Properties: Dance, movement

Although the mimosa was originally found in southwestern and eastern Asia, Theophrastus confuses it for acanthus in his writing. Clearly, the tree was well known to many early civilizations.

Currently, the tree is being banned in many areas due to its wispy tendrils. These tendrils clog filters in air conditioners and cars and cause overheating. Further, the feathered seeds affect those who suffer from breathing conditions, and the heptanoic acid causes the tree to emit a putrid smell, which further causes distress.

In the Magical Circle: Movement

While you may use the mimosa in a ritual to enhance movement either to or from somewhere or someone, the mimosa also works well as a talisman. The mimosa is a wonderful tree to make a broom out of if you or one of your coven members is a dancer or does a lot of movement, such as gymnastics, sports, or running track. To assist you in your movement endeavors, take a whisk broom of mimosa with you as you perform whatever sport or activity you choose. You may even leave the broom in your bag where its energy will pass onto that which you wear or use in your endeavor.

Working with Mimosa

Mimosa is very hard to work, and it's heavy, wet or dry, so be prepared for some workouts just getting the wood to the bench or lathe. The grain is gray and has a strange stringiness to it that gives it an almost marble-like quality. All of this doesn't mean you shouldn't work with mimosa. It's a very pretty wood when sealed or stained, and the heftiness of the wood gives a solidity to a broom whether in circle or in the house. Of the many woods Chelsea has worked with, she recommends mimosa if not for the above characteristics, then for the sheer joy of seeing the grain come to life.

Mulberry

Order: Rosales
Family: Moraceae
Genus: *Morus*
Species: *alba* (white), *nigra* (black), *rubra* (red)
Energy: Masculine
Frequency: 74
Element: Air
Gods: Fei Lian, Fujin
Goddess: Kichijoten
Properties: Love, passion

The mulberry comes in three varieties: white, red, and black. When we think of them, we both think of Labrador retrievers. They come in black, yellow, or chocolate, but they are all Labs. It's the same with the mulberry. The only difference is the color of their fruit. Any of the three are perfect for wine making, jams, or jellies.

In the Magical Circle: Finding Love

The berries are also reputed to be good for love potions, but neither of us personally know anything about that, so we cannot say for certain. However, if you wish to perform a love or passion ritual with your mulberry broom, then any of the three species will work the same. Remember, for any love magic, do not attempt to force your passion or your will on someone else lest it come back to you.

For use in ritual, take your mulberry broom, a red candle, a white candle, and a glass of clean water. Place everything on the altar. Open the circle as you would with whatever you usually use. Once the circle is open, start at east, the beginning of everything, and sweep inward in a clockwise circle.

Once you have done that, light the white candle and present it to each quarter starting with east. Then leave the lit candle on the altar and light the red candle. Take that candle to all four quarters also. Back at the altar, press the two lit candles together. Let the wax mix as you take both candles around one more time.

Say something only if you want to. Once you have the intertwined wax of the two candles on the altar, take the glass of clean water and sprinkle it as you again walk around the circle. This time, say as you walk, "I cleanse this circle so that love may grow from two hearts into one with acceptance and agreement, and without binds, clasps, or conditions."

When back at the altar, place both lit candles into the glass of water and let them burn to the level of the water and then extinguish themselves. Now, take your mulberry broom and sweep once again into the circle from the east, welcoming the new love that has been joined. Close the circle as you wish. Once the circle has been closed, bury what is left of the water and the candles at the base of a mulberry, cherry, or apple tree. You have asked for love and planted the magical seed for love to grow.

Working with Mulberry

Mulberry is like hackberry. It works well, is clear of a lot of knots, and you can work it until it is cured and then as it hardens. Keep your tools sharp and your resolve strong and you'll have a great broom that you will love.

Oak

Order: Fagales
Family: Fagaceae
Genus: *Quercus*
Species: spp.
Energy: Masculine
Frequency: 55
Elements: Air, fire
Gods: Cernunnos, Herne, Thor, Zeus
Goddesses: Artemis, Brigid, Ceridwen, the Morrigan, Diana
Property: Strength

The oak is a multispecies tree. There are approximately 435 species of oaks in the world. In the United States, there are approximately 90 of those species. Most oaks are deciduous, which means they drop their leaves in the winter; however, the live oak that is prevalent in the southern states is an evergreen oak. It retains a majority of its leaves on the tree but does drop some.

With the vast array of oaks in the wild, it is not surprising that the oak is a sought-after wood for building, crafting, and ornamental use. The red and white oak are easy to find in many dimensions at big-box lumber stores, and furniture made of oak is still being used after hundreds of years and is often available at antique shops and flea markets.

In the Magical Circle: Strength

All oaks are equally powerful magically and make a strong and useful broom when cleaning or sweeping—not always the same thing, either in or out of circle. If you need an added push in your ritual, or if your spell is not going where you need it to go, cast with an oak wand. If you don't have an oak wand, then use your oak broom for all ritual work. Once the circle is opened, take your oak broom from the altar and sweep the circle inward starting from north, the guardian of strength. As you walk the circle in a clockwise direction, sweep either inward if you need help with your ritual or outward if you are trying to remove a roadblock to success. Complete your ritual and then close the circle with the oak wand or oak broom as your tradition teaches.

Working with Oak

Oak is another wood that is much easier to work green than dry. The wood is very strong, and when dried, it makes a perfect broom handle since it is so resilient and naturally grained. It's a great wood for many things and gives the broom great strength when you are using it in circle.

Olive

Order: Lamiales
Family: Oleaceae
Genus: *Olea*
Species: *europaea*
Energy: Masculine
Frequency: 76
Elements: All four
Gods: Apollo, Hercules, Horus, Ra, Zeus
Goddesses: Athena, Amaterasu, Minerva
Property: Purity

One would think, and one would be wrong, that olive trees are not prevalent in most parts of the United States. With big-box garden stores and specialty nurseries, the olive tree is showing up in more gardens and backyards than you may think. And with those thousands of trees, there will be many failed attempts at keeping them alive. And here is where you get a sought-after broom handle: the olive.

In the Magical Circle: Purity

Using an olive broom in circle is for those who are looking for purity and chastity. Neither of these may be of the physical nature, but then again, they might be. You don't need to cast a circle with your olive broom. Wherever you need that purity in your life—in your home, your workspace, your relationship—that is where the broom should be kept. Above a door, on your desk, or under your bed, whisk brooms are best for that due to size.

Working with Olive

The only olive wood either of us have ever had of any size was enough to make a wand, and that was using sandpaper and a carving knife. Therefore, we will leave you with the same advice we give everyone: Take it slow. Take it easy. And do whatever you will with respect and resolve.

It's also important when making an olive broom to be as clean, chaste, and pure as possible. Now, we're not advocating that only virgins make olive brooms. But we are saying that when you craft an olive broom, take special care to be cognizant of your surroundings. Do it in a clean space. Remember this is the tree of purity.

Cast a circle before working on your broom to keep negative energies from your work area, and if you don't finish in one session, which you won't, close the circle and cast again each time. The broom will know and appreciate it.

Orange

Order: Sapindales
Family: Rutaceae
Genus: *Citrus*
Species: ×*sinensis*
Energy: Masculine
Frequency: 83
Element: Fire
God: Cupid
Goddess: Venus
Properties: Health, romance, love

Gypsey loves orange wood because the smell of the fresh wood is unlike any other wood in this list. However, in Florida there have been a few outbreaks of disease with the orange groves, so finding large pieces will require you to source your wood locally. That's not a problem if you know people who have old trees that they are looking to remove. Usually, a friend of a friend is all it takes. But if you don't live in the Deep South where there are orange trees in almost every neighborhood, you may have to search a little more.

The utility of the orange is that of all other citrus fruits: vitamin C. Scurvy was rampant on the long voyages of tall ships because of the lack of vitamin C in the crews' diets. In 1747, James Lind proved that citrus juice, combined with other nutrients, was a cure and precaution against scurvy. Aboard the HMS Salisbury, Lind conducted the first experiment on sailors and showed that the juices of oranges and lemons would counteract the debilitating condition.

A broom of orange will be scented for years if you don't seal it. And there are some strains of orange (unfortunately, not the ones commercially grown) that have a slight orange tinge to the wood.

In the Magical Circle: Romance

Using an orange broom around your home will enhance your success in love and romance. In circle, the orange broom will also help grant you great success in love and romance. Follow the ritual suggestions for cherry.

Working with Orange

As with any citrus, the wood is very clean and workable. Even after the wood dries, it remains easy to work and soft to the touch. While that may be a boon in one aspect: more work time in the shop, it is a bane in another area: the wood will gouge or mar if you are not careful even after it becomes a broom. Please be careful.

Osage Orange

Order: Rosales
Family: Moraceae
Genus: *Maclura*
Species: *pomifera*
Energies: Feminine and masculine
Frequency: 93
Element: Earth
God: Wah'kon-tah
Goddess: Wah'kon-tah
Property: Ancestral magic

Gypsey spent over twenty years in Oklahoma and got to know the Osage orange trees very well. As a landscape architect, when not calling them out by genus and species, she also referred to them as the *bois d'arc* tree, which is the French word for "bow wood." However, to add more confusion, the locals also just call them horse apples, which is silly since the horses don't eat the fruit and you shouldn't either. While it won't specifically kill you, the pains you will get in your gut will make you wish it did.

We both, though, think that the Osage orange is the best wood to make a broom handle out of because in time it darkens to a very lovely orange, just like its name. A broom of Osage orange will last you a lifetime and your children and grandchildren their lifetimes. Chelsea knows of farmers in Oklahoma who have Osage fence posts in their fields that their great-grandfathers put in the ground.

In the Magical Circle: Ancestral Magic

An Osage orange broom in circle will bring you and your ancestors together better than any other broom. We wouldn't recommend this broom for divination, but if you wish to contact the Earth Mother or the All Spirit, then this is the broom for you. Divine with the Osage orange by following the ritual in chapter 5. Be prepared, though, for what you encounter. The Earth Mother is not to be trifled with. She can be nurturing as well as punishing. Depends on who you are and what you want.

In a ritual or circle, you are not casting with your Osage orange broom. Instead, place a fifth altar in the center with just the broom on it. Once the circle is opened in whatever manner your group or you decide, go to the broom and pick it up. Holding it loosely in your hands, any way that is comfortable for you, think through the broom out into the void and ask whatever question or wish you have of whatever ancestor you are attempting to contact. If you have trouble standing, then a chair is suggested. Be alert to the nuances that may come to you. Ancestors do not always speak in ways we may understand.

When you have received whatever message you need or want, then thank your ancestors and wish them a pleasant and safe journey back to their realm. Then, place the broom back on the small table or altar and resume your ritual or circle.

Working with Osage Orange

The wood is soft and easy to work until it dries completely. We know we say that about a lot of woods, and this one is among them. You can still do carving, woodworking, or other fine work on a dried Osage orange. Just be aware that when the wood is dry, you will have to work around the knots and harder spots. A friend once made a set of runes with ebony and inset the runes in Osage orange from a post in his back field that was over ninety years old. He swore he would never work with either wood again since both were well dried. Either wet or dry, the outcome will be most satisfying. Enjoy the process.

Padauk (African Variety)

Order: Fabales
Family: Fabaceae
Genus: *Pterocarpus*
Species: *soyauxii*
Energy: Female
Frequency: 5
Element: Fire
God: Nyambe
Goddesses: Ala, Anyanwu
Properties: Dark energy, protection
Warning: Causes skin irritation to those susceptible to rashes from plants like poison ivy.

Padauk is a beautiful wood for whisks, short brooms, or, if you are able to get a piece in the raw, for full brooms. The red hues are often used for musical instruments, and it shines up nicely when sealed.

While not as highly toxic as poison ivy, the dust and shavings of padauk wood will cause a similar effect on your skin and respiratory system. However, that notwithstanding, the wood is amazing for protection. A broom of padauk will keep you warded and protected like nothing else, other than its darker big brother, poison ivy.

When Gypsey first worked with this wood, she was not aware of the aggravation the dust would cause to the skin. She made many of her wands on a lathe and did so with this wood. She had a couple of holes in her long-sleeved shirt and some burn holes in the stomach area from doing forge work. After she cleaned up, she didn't take any precautions that she would have with poison ivy and went golfing. After nine holes, she came home to shower and had small rashes exactly where the holes in her clothing were. This is the power of the powder of the padauk.

In the Magical Circle: Protection

As we said, this wood is a dark-energy wood. It will protect you, but it will also respond if you are using the tool as a weapon. We as witches have the power to be both protective and aggressive. And even though the threefold rule applies when one uses a tool in an aggressive manner, some do it nonetheless.

When using a padauk broom, it's best to cast a circle for your protection rather than attacking an individual you are dealing with. Place your broom in the southern quarter. After casting your circle as you normally would, pick up your padauk broom from the southern quarter altar, hold it with outstretched arms, if you can, and, starting at south, walk the circle in a clockwise direction with the bristles pointing upward.

As you walk the circle, call out to your deities to channel their energies through the padauk broom and form a protective shield around you. Once back at south, place the broom on the southern quarter altar and continue with your ritual.

Working with Padauk

As noted above, be careful with this wood. It doesn't have the oils that poison ivy does, and it's doubtful you will ever be able to find a raw piece of it outside of Africa, so the wood will most likely be kiln or air dried to remove any sap, but it's still dangerous. Dress in goggles, long-sleeved shirt, gloves, long pants, and old shoes. Strip after working with it and shower. Jewelweed soap works very well with urushiol oil from poison ivy and should work well for you to wash away the padauk dust. If you are unable to find jewelweed soap, most good soaps and shampoos should clean you off as well. To be certain though, wash twice.

Again, we recommend you work at the dark moon from ten o'clock at night to two o'clock in the morning. We also recommend you cast a circle and ask for assistance from your deities to get the job done. Concentrate on why you are making this tool and what you want to do with it. This and poison ivy are pretty much the only two woods that you need to be very specific about your intentions with since most of the others are very loose in their assistance. This wood is not. It is directed. It wants to know what it's going to do. It wants to get a chance to do it. And it will revel in the accomplishment once the task is completed.

Finally, enjoy this broom. It's beautiful. It looks good on the wall and will shine in the sun. Just don't forget that it's not one of your bright and shiny pieces. It does its job. And so should you.

Peach

Order: Rosales
Family: Rosaceae
Genus: *Prunus*
Species: *persica*
Energy: Feminine
Frequency: 82
Element: Earth
God: Momotaro
Goddess: Venus
Properties: Steadiness, exorcism

The peach is similar to all other non-citrus fruit trees. Anything either of us said about the apple, or the pear below, will also be true about the peach and the plum. Peach pits and walnut shells have become popular again for carvings and creating miniature dioramas in them. It takes a steady hand to accomplish these feats, and the peach is a good tree because it also gives steadiness with use.

In the Magical Circle: Exorcism

The peach broom is useful if you are trying to rid yourself of anything, either positive or negative.

Once the circle is open, take the peach broom and hold it vertical at arm's length with the handle end of the broom at eye level. While walking around the circle from the north, call out what you are attempting to exorcise in your life. Make certain that you stop at all the quarters and repeat three times what you wish to be rid of. Once back at north, turn the broom so that the ends of the bristles are at eye level and do the same ritual again. This process sends the energy of the broom through to the ground and up to the aether.

Working with Peach

Peach is as easy to work as any of the other fruit trees. It is worked best wet, but it is relatively easy to work with even dry. The smell of the wood is very pleasant, and it will enhance your work area with the aroma. However, make certain your tools are very sharp. Since this wood is soft, even when dry, it will gouge easily if your tools are not sharp and your hands are not steady.

Pear

Order: Rosales
Family: Rosaceae
Genus: *Pyrus*
Species: *communis*
Energy: Feminine
Frequency: 82
Element: Water
God: Cernunnos
Goddesses: Venus, Aphrodite, Hera, Pomona
Properties: Love, lust

There are many types of pears: the European edible version and the Bradford, which is now being banned due to its invasiveness, are but two of them. The Bradford has a tendency to distribute its tendrils into air conditioning vents and car air filters, causing overheating and expensive repair bills. Further, the feathered seeds, similar to the cottonwood, may affect breathing for those who suffer from breathing conditions. Therefore, we will discuss the European pear, often called the Bartlett.

In the Magical Circle: Marriage

The pear is an excellent wood for love and lust—again, often not the same thing. Pear brooms are perfect for jumping in handfasting ceremonies. See the handfasting ritual in chapter 7.

Working with Pear

All fruit trees may be lumped together. They are rather soft, rather attractive, and rather easy to work with. They have grains that vary from striated to mottled, and it depends on which you are looking for. For our money, though, we would both go with cherry over any of the other fruits other than plum, which if you get a *Prunus cerasifera*, is a deep purple. However, choices are always up to the individual, and the pear is a lovely broom to add to your magical array.

Pecan

Order: Fagales
Family: Juglandaceae
Genus: *Carya*
Species: *illinoinensis*
Energy: Masculine
Frequency: 82
Element: Air
God: Mercury
Goddess: Priapus
Properties: Money, employment

The pecan tree is one of the many nut trees in the US and other countries. The word *pecan* is from an Algonquian word meaning "requiring a stone to crack," coming from the fact that the nut is very hard to crack to get to the meat inside. The tree is native from as far west as Iowa and Indiana and as far south as Alabama, Texas, and into Mexico.[34] Tree farms may be seen in many states, and the trees are well separated to allow the vibration machines to shake the trees to release the mature nuts. They're planted in perfect rows for easy weeding, watering, and access.

In the Magical Circle: Money

Magically, the wood is a powerful money and employment symbol. Take your pecan broom and anoint it with either money-draw oil or wealth oil, usually available at metaphysical bookstores or online. Tie a green ribbon around the handle and hang it in the vicinity of your work or office space.

34. Michael Dirr, *Manual of Woody Landscape Plants: Their Identification, Ornamental Characteristics, Culture, Propagation and Uses*, 6th ed. (Stipes Publishing, 2009), 212.

Working with Pecan

Pecan is a great wood to work with. It's rather heavy, and the wood reflects the great strength of the spirit of the tree. Pecan takes a while to dry, so don't rush it, and work it green. It will gouge and mar when green though, and if you are not careful, you will end up with an ugly piece of firewood. Ironically, when the wood dries, it becomes very hard, and then you have the problem of making certain your tools are as sharp as possible if you waited too long. It's rather an either-or situation, with one option being too soft and one option being too hard. Unlike the story of Goldilocks, there is no third option.

Persimmon

Order: Ericales
Family: Ebenaceae
Genus: *Diospyros*
Species: *virginiana*
Energies: Feminine and masculine
Frequency: 80
Element: Water
God: Hermaphroditus
Goddess: Hermaphroditus
Property: Gender fluidity

In the United States, the prevalent persimmon is the *virginiana*. In the areas of the Mediterranean, you will find the *Diospyros lotus*. The fruit is sweet and good for jams and jellies, but make certain you use fully ripened fruit. Unripe fruit has been known to cause severe stomach ailments. Additionally, never eat persimmons on an empty stomach because without a food base, even a tiny amount of the chemicals may be unpleasant.

The Mediterranean species was mentioned in Homer's *Odyssey* as the fruit eaten in the land of the lotus-eaters. Further, the word *persimmon* is thought to be of Powhatan origin, though the word in other forms is found prior to the European expansion to North America.

In the Magical Circle: Duality

Magically, the persimmon is sacred to the deity Hermaphroditus and is equally at home in either a male or female ritual. To use persimmon is to evoke the duality of the individual spirit. With a persimmon broom you may sweep both masculine and feminine energy either into or out of your ritual. If you want the dual energies in your circle, begin at the eastern quarter and sweep inward, moving in a clockwise direction. If you want the dual energies removed from your circle, begin at the western quarter and sweep outward while moving in a counterclockwise direction. When completed with either sweeping, return the broom to the main altar and continue your ritual.

Working with Persimmon

When you are working with persimmon, it is brittle. Care needs to be taken to make certain you cut the entire limb when coppicing the branch or you run the chance of pulling the bark up the limb and ruining the look of the broom handle. Once the wood is prepared and you start working it, you will notice a sweet smell to the wood from the sap, and the grain is quite clear and well laid out. If you work the wood green, which is a better way to do it, wait for the wood to fully dry before attempting to sand it. The green wood will gum up your sanding belts or papers and you will frustrate yourself more than necessary.

Pine

Order: Pinales
Family: Pinaceae
Genus: *Pinus*
Species: *strobus* (white), *sylvestris* (Scots)
Energy: Masculine
Frequency: 51
Element: Air
God: Pan
Goddesses: Astarte, Venus
Property: Fertility

Everyone knows the pine. Either the white (*strobus*) or the Scots (*sylvestris*) wood are in every big-box, little-box, and large hardware chain store across the country. The pine is found all across the United States and in many foreign countries. Depending on the climate, the pine will differ to adjust to dry, wet, hot, or cold climates. The Bahamian pine has developed with a very high canopy of limbs to avoid being destroyed in the dry fires that burn throughout the Bahamas. They are indicated by high, limbless trunks with a crop of limbs on top, much like a lollipop.

In the Magical Circle: Fertility

In magical circles, there is little the pine is good for other than fertility, which in itself is pretty important. Actually, cast the circle with your pine broom starting at east, where all things are conceived. Call the quarters as you would with a wand or athame. Then, with your partner, hold hands and state with the broom on the altar that you wish to conceive. Once the circle is concluded, you or your partner will close the circle, again from east and also walking clockwise. Once the circle is completed, go home or wherever you are doing your conception attempt and place the broom at the head of the bed, blanket, sleeping bag, etc., and leave it there during coitus.

Working with Pine

Pine is the easiest wood to work with. Wet, dry, green, seasoned—it's going to work the same way. The yellow pine is harder to work with because the yellow pine tree has many branches that cause knots in the wood. That's the reason it's so inexpensive for building projects and also why you usually end up painting it to cover the knots. White pine has few branches, and the wood is much whiter, giving a cleaner look to whatever you are building. Brooms, though, don't care. Either variety will work as well as the other, and it depends only on whether you want a knotty broom handle or a smooth and cleaner-looking one.

Pine is happy to help you achieve whatever you wish to do with it. If pine was a dog, we'd liken it to a cocker spaniel puppy: all bounce and joy.

Plum (Purple Leaf)

Order: Rosales
Family: Rosaceae
Genus: *Prunus*
Species: *cerasifera*
Energy: Feminine
Frequency: 82
Element: Water
Gods: Liber, Picumnus
Goddess: Venus
Properties: Cleaning, being a specimen broom

This tree is beautiful. The bark, the leaves, and the fruit are all purple. In the front yard of a house, it just looks perfect. The only issue we have with the plum is that it is susceptible to a few varieties of wood-boring insects. If the tree is not treated regularly, the insects will get into the wood and rot the tree. We've seen it happen a number of times, and it was always sad to see a beautiful plum tree be taken down with tree rot. These trees may be purchased at many specialty nurseries and will add a splash of color to your front yard.

In the Magical Circle: Specimen Broom

There are no recommendations for using this broom in circle. As some live trees are specimen trees, the purple leaf plum is a specimen broom. The broom is the object of attention, and once the wood dries, it takes on a darkish orange hue even though you would expect it to remain purple. We would definitely recommend sealing this broom just to be safe and to hopefully keep the beautiful hue for years to come.

Working with Purple Leaf Plum

If you work the wood green, then you will have good success with your tools. And if you are making a short whisk or turkey broom, then you will have good fortune using a lathe. Even dry, the wood is easy to work and won't cause you any trouble like some other woods like locust or hornbeam do.

Poison Ivy

Order: Sapindales
Family: Anacardiaceae
Genus: *Toxicodendron*
Species: *radicans*
Energy: Feminine
Frequency: 1
Elements: Earth, fire
Gods: Pluto, Ra, Thoth
Goddess: Hel
Property: Dark magic
Warning: Poison ivy is very dangerous to those susceptible to it. Extreme caution should be taken when using this wood.

Poison ivy may be found all over the United States. It is recognized by three shiny leaves of the same size. The plant grows to be exceptionally thick and hearty if left to itself. We have seen vines more than 3 inches in diameter and ones that have overgrown full-sized trees.

When dealing with this vine, be exceptionally cautious. The oils will remain long after the wood has been cut and worked. If you attempt to rid yourself of this vine, don't use commercial weed killer. Remember, weed killer kills everything—not just the weed you are spraying. Get goats. Get sheep. Rent them if necessary.

In the Magical Circle: Anything It Wants

For every other wood in these sections, we have given you a ritual or a use. Poison ivy is the exception. You may use this tool for any ritual. Just remember that it is pure dark energy, so whatever you are trying to accomplish will always tend to turn that way. Healing rituals and love magic are probably not a good idea. This wood likes to stick to protection, reversals of spells, and things that other wands shun. However, poison ivy will get the job done.

Working with Poison Ivy

Poison ivy is not a warm and fuzzy plant to work with. It can kill you. Let us make that perfectly clear at the outset. And it's not for those who shy away from the dark energy of the Craft. This plant, which is a vine but will grow to amazing thickness and sturdiness, is there for the using if you are willing, able, and cognizant of how to do that.

Gypsey is deathly allergic to poison ivy. However, with that knowledge, she still works with it and achieves some amazing results. The vine is beautiful once it's dried, although it may take up to five years for the urushiol to dry, and even then, the residue may be toxic until, well, no one knows. The grain is dark when the vine gets large enough to be used as a whisk or short broom. And when dried, properly sanded, and preserved with a fine wood oil, the vine will shine and show off the sheer power it possesses.

There is no turning back once you work with this wood. The antithesis of holly, which can do nothing dark, poison ivy is incapable of doing anything light. It is a dark-energy wood, and that's the bottom line. To best derive the energy from this wood, it is recommended that you prepare it at the darkest of the moon between the hours of 10 o'clock at night and 2 o'clock in the morning. You get one shot at this per month. But it's okay if you don't finish your work. You can always pick it up again the next month. The wood will be there for you and will wait patiently for you to complete your task.

Gypsey made a wand of poison ivy one time for a customer. She wanted it very badly for protection magic but was highly allergic to the plant. Even when she handled the sealed box the wand was in, she said she could feel the energy through her latex gloves. That's when she asked if the wand would work while she was protected. Gypsey commented that if she could feel the energy through the latex and the protective plastic, then Gypsey was certain she could use the wand through latex. She did and it worked perfectly. This is the same with a whisk or short broom. Even if you are highly allergic to the wood and the oil, you can still navigate the dark energies by applying some precautions to your ritual.

Before we give you some helpful hints on how to work with the wood, remember that the wood is there both for you and not for you. You may work in conjunction with this wood or you may fight it. Either way, poison ivy is going to win. This is the one wood you cannot control, merely ride alongside it and kindly ask it to help you. It will. It enjoys its place on the spectrum of energy. It should. It's the king to holly's queen.

There are two ways to work with poison ivy: wet or dry. If you have the time, and few of us do anymore, you can wait till it naturally dries, which, as we said above, may take up to five-plus years. Or you can work the wood fresh and wet.

First, wear protective gear. We don't just mean gloves. That's a given. We also mean a face mask, long-sleeved shirt, long pants, socks, and old shoes. Try to keep as much of your skin protected as possible. Wear a respirator. When you are working in a closed space, the oil can become airborne and aggravate your lungs. Do not have moving air. You don't want a fan or an open window or door—nothing that can put the pieces into the atmosphere and allow them to settle on you. Use hand tools. Avoid anything mechanical because it may cause the pieces to fly around your work area. And whatever you do: Don't work in the house!

Now, figure out what you want to make. That may seem obvious, but it's amazing how many people change their mind in the middle of a project. This is not one of those woods you want to do that to. Work slowly and methodically. You have a four-hour window, and you can get a lot accomplished in that time frame.

As with many of the other projects, cast a circle around your work area. Call any specific gods and goddesses to be with you, and if you are creating this tool for a specific reason, ask them to imbue the piece with the necessary energies and protections for you. This is not a tool to be bandied about on the wall. This is a weapon of either offensive or defensive magic and will respond to what you wish it to do.

When you are done for the night, and it will usually take you more than one session to finish this unless you are a skilled woodworker or just plain driven, put the piece in a safe place. We both have special boxes that we store our poison ivy in. They are lockable, although neither of us ever lock them. They are in a cool and dry place and are out of the way of anyone who might bump into them, which has never happened since our households are all Pagan and Heathen.

When you're finished working for the night, strip in the laundry room and put your clothes in the washer immediately. You don't want to leave any residual oil anywhere around the house. Go directly to the shower and scrub. If you can find jewelweed soap, then use it. It's as good as they claim it is. If not, then scrub with a good body soap and wash everything twice.

We both love and hate working with poison ivy. The results are amazing, but the process is precarious at best. As an aside, when Gypsey used to do poison ivy wands once a year, she would call her doctor and tell her, "I'm going to the woods." Her doctor would immediately call in a heavy-duty prescription of prednisone for Gypsey, and Gypsey scheduled the dark moon night at the height of her prescription. This didn't work all the time but it did help.

Poplar

Order: Malpighiales
Family: Salicaceae
Genus: *Populus*
Species: *tremuloides*
Energy: Masculine
Frequency: 50
Elements: Air, water
God: Tyr
Goddess: Hecate
Properties: Generic broom, entry to the underworld

Even though we think of willow as the go-to tree for medicinal bark, the poplar's bark also contains salicin, although not to the same degree. Poplars have amazing regenerative powers. The multiple roots will regrow quickly after devastating forest fires.

In the Magical Circle: The Underworld

When Gypsey gave lectures on wood and their energies, people would ask if there is a wood that does everything, magickally speaking. That wood is poplar. The only problem with poplar is that even though it can do everything, it does nothing well. So if you want a good broom to give to your students, your non-magical friends, or those you don't trust with powerful energies, then give them a poplar broom. They will use it and enjoy it and won't cause any metaphysical chaos if they attempt to do something they shouldn't.

A poplar broom is ideal for protection circles against fire or for quick recovery. Further, with a poplar broom you can sweep a path to the underworld. Be cautious of that, though, and treat that ritual with great care. For if you fail to leave yourself a way back, then you will be there forever. Toward the end of the incantation to the underworld, make certain you state that you are a visitor to that realm and that while you enjoy visiting, you do not wish to be a permanent resident of the underworld. When it is time to conclude, thank the gods that you met there and then thank them for allowing you to visit, and then leave.

As we have said, poplar is a generic wood. It will do anything you ask of it and, therefore, will respond to whatever you attempt to do to it in the shop. However, if you expect more than that, you are fooling yourself. You just won't get it, so don't wait for it.

Working with Poplar

Poplar is a nice wood to work with. It's not too hard, not too soft, not too grainy, and not too clean. It works moderately well with hand tools and moderately well with power tools. You may work it during the day or at night. There is no better moon cycle to work poplar. If this sounds like a commercial for a middle-of-the-road wood, then you are absolutely correct. Poplar is exactly that: middle of the road.

Privet

Order: Lamiales
Family: Oleaceae
Genus: *Ligustrum*
Species: spp.
Energy: Masculine
Frequency: 32
Element: Earth
Gods: Brahma, Vishnu
Goddesses: Lakshmi, Parvati
Property: Separation

The privet is a shrub rather than a tree, although in some species in China and the Himalayas it may grow to tree height. It is best known in the United States for being the hedgerow between houses in subdivisions and along roadways. The shrub is often cut boxlike, and in the fall, there are plenty of insects and birds feeding on the small berries that the shrub produces.

In the Magical Circle: Separation

Privet brooms are excellent for separating things. Much as a winnow sieve works with grain, the privet broom will separate the "wheat" from the "chaff" in a decision. Instead of casting a circle with the broom, place it in front of you in a dimly lit room and look into the bristles. Concentrate on what you are attempting to separate and see the decisions before you. When you see the one that makes the most sense and gives the optimum outcome, then thank the gods and goddesses and follow your decision to its conclusion.

Working with Privet

It can be hard to find a large-enough privet to make a broom handle from, but if you do, it is a wonderful wood to make a broom from. Gypsey has a privet short broom that Chelsea's mentor made her years ago. It hangs behind the couch. It isn't expected to do anything but look good. Which it does exceptionally well. Privet wood is very hard and dense and relatively straight. You can create some beautiful effects if you peel the rather uninteresting bark, leaving some of the rich, red under bark over the clear, light wood. As always, allow to dry thoroughly before using.

Rosemary

Order: Lamiales
Family: Lamiaceae
Genus: *Rosmarinus*
Species: *officinalis*
Energy: Masculine
Frequency: 95
Element: Fire
God: Vulcan
Goddess: Aphrodite
Property: Lightning magic

Rosemary is not a shrub or wood you would think of for a broom, even a short whisk one. However, the shrub is surprising in that respect. While the finer limbs are thin and spindly, the central shaft is incredibly durable and quite robust. The wood is very hard for a soft evergreen shrub and when allowed to grow to almost dieback stage is large enough to make a fine little handle for a whisk.

In the Magical Circle: Electrical Magic

The unusual characteristic of this wood is its ability to carry electrical magic. We have found that working with weather energy and weather magic is exceptionally successful when using rosemary. The wood, though, is also very adept at health and healing magic and will allow the user of the broom to sweep away toxins and health issues when used in circle.

We recommend that you draw energy from the sky and the storm to energize whatever you need done in your ritual. In circle, use the broom—and we mean a whisk broom since it's unlikely you will be able to ever get a full-length broom handle out of a rosemary—and open the circle as you would with a wand. The best time for this ritual and circle is when there is heat lightning or diffused lightning around you. Do not attempt to operate a circle or ritual in a full-blown thunderstorm unless you are certain the storm is far enough away as to not be attracted by your magic. And there is no way to guarantee that. So let's just not do it. Stay safe with what people refer to as *heat lightning* and conclude your business. Sometime during the ritual, hold the rosemary broom above your head and call to your deities to empower this broom with the necessary energies for what you have set out to do. Once your energy has been acquired, close the circle. We have found that being safely under cover is the perfect place to watch the celestial light show once the ritual is concluded.

Working with Rosemary

When crafting a rosemary broom, you should plan to do it during a thunderstorm. A day storm of intense energy works very well, and you don't have to worry about the phase of the moon as you do with some other tools you are making.

We like using small hand or power tools. The grain is interesting in that the wood is rather pale, almost dirty white, but there are many little pockmarks in the central shaft where the smaller limbs grew out. Don't try to sand or cut them out. Just work with them. They give the wood a really nice character and provide a grip that you don't often get with a regular round shafted whisk or broom.

Rowan

Order: Rosales
Family: Rosaceae
Genus: *Sorbus*
Species: spp.
Energy: Feminine
Frequency: 97
Elements: Earth, fire
Gods: Thor, Vulcan
Goddesses: Aphrodite, Brigid, Ceridwen, Hebe, Hecate
Properties: Ancestor magic, request magic

Rowan will be the hardest wood to find in this book. It is not a wood that is harvested for any particular purpose, and almost every witch we know wants a wand of rowan. So whatever you do find will be snatched up quickly by others. In the South, it's called *mountain ash*.

There is a wood and paneling shop in Atlanta, Georgia. It's in an old gas station between a Burger King and a McDonalds, and you would pass it if you didn't know what you were looking for. For years, Gypsey had a standing order that if they ever got rowan in, she wanted the first shot at it. One afternoon, they called her at work to say they had two bundles of rowan. She left work immediately and drove the ninety minutes to Atlanta from Clemson to get it. When she drove up, one of the young lads put two bundles of limbs in the back of her truck without even asking. She said to him, "I don't need all of that." He replied, "Doesn't matter. You're going to pay for all of them anyway." Such was working with our wood people that could find rowan. And by the way, she did pay for both bundles.

In the Magical Circle: Magical Requests

Rowan is best when left to its own devices. By that I mean use the broom in circle and merely ask it to do whatever you need it to do. You don't have to be overly articulate because the rowan is overly observant. It will see what you need and provide. Start in the south. Cast your circle clockwise. Begin the circle by asking the broom to provide what it is you need. Asking it for what you want isn't always best for you. The broom will know. Conduct your circle as you would from the south, walking clockwise. When closing, again go from south and again walk clockwise. Thank the broom for what it will bring you that you need. And when your need arrives, thank the broom. You don't have to be elaborate. Just a thank-you is enough. The broom will be expecting it.

Working with Rowan

It's a fifty-fifty shot that you will find green rowan. Either wet or dry, the rowan will work well if you have good tools and a calm and steady hand. It is best to craft your broom at the full moon. You don't have to work at night for this one, just within the twenty-four hours of that full moon day and night. Hand tools are best if you have that ability. The rowan appreciates the "hands on" approach. If you have dexterity issues, then the wood will understand and allow you to use whatever you are capable of.

Spruce

Order: Pinales
Family: Pinaceae
Genus: *Picea*
Species: *sitchensis*
Energy: Feminine
Frequency: 66
Elements: Earth, water
God: Poseidon
Goddesses: Ceridwen, Cybele
Property: Broom construction techniques

There are many spruce types, and we are going to focus on Sitka spruce. It is the largest of the spruce trees and the easiest to find. While you probably won't find it in your local lumberyard in Florida or Texas, it's readily available in the upper states, Western Canada, and Alaska. Sitka spruce is another wood that is best confined to sweeping the house or the shop rather than being used in circle, where it can get confused easily and not give you what you need. While not as generic as poplar, it is still close to the center of usefulness.

In the Magical Circle: Construction

If you are building something—a house, a barn, a shed, a workshop, a fence—this is the broom you want to have handy. There isn't a ritual designed for this. However, have the broom with you. Use it to clean up, either before or after your work. Keep the broom close as you complete your project and then enjoy it. The broom will have a vested interest in the project and will want to be part of it after being introduced.

Working with Spruce

Spruce is a great wood to make a broom from since the branches are large enough to easily be crafted into full broom handles. The bark will peel off easily with just a sharp woodworking knife, and there is little left to do to make the broom.

Do as you will. There isn't much you can do to harm the wood, and it's easy enough that you can use this wood, if you can get enough of it, to teach budding broom makers.

Sumac

Order: Sapindales
Family: Anacardiaceae
Genus: *Rhus*
Species: *coriaria*
Energy: Masculine
Frequency: 52
Element: Fire
God: Huehueteotl
Goddesses: Cihuacoatl, Chantico
Property: Connection

Tree sumac is not poison sumac. While they are both called sumac, they are different genera and species. The tree sumac has large amounts of small, red fruit during the fall and may grow 8–10 feet tall. While most people in the US do not use the fruit, only enjoying the fall color, in the Middle East, the fruit is dried, ground, and used as a spice.

In the Magical Circle: Connection

Magically, sumac is a connecting wood. It is used as a nexus between fire, its base element, and the Earth or Mother Goddess. It may be said that sumac is the intermediary between Pele and Gaia.

Use a broom of sumac to open circle from the south. Another member of the ritual takes a broom or wand of magnolia and does the same from north. Concurrently, they begin walking clockwise, opening the circle at each quarter in unison. Either may start and the other may finish at each quarter. Just make that decision before the ritual. Once back at their respective positions, they lay their broom on their starting quarters and begin the ritual.

This ritual is a liaison between fire and earth. True, they are both of the planet; however, often they seem diametrically opposed. The earth brings bounty, and the fire, at times, destroys that by creating new. In the circle, request that the deities work with each other and not negate the other's accomplishments. Iceland and Hawai'i both come to mind with this ritual. Both islands were formed from volcanoes. Both islands have new land being added yearly by lava flows at the expense of crops, property, and already-created land. This ritual works to form a beneficial cooperative for the betterment of those affected.

When the ritual is completed, repeat the opening in reverse. Each person takes their broom and, walking counterclockwise from their starting quarter, presents the brooms and thanks the deities present for attending and hopefully assisting. Then, close the circle as you would by walking counterclockwise, releasing the quarters as you pass them. Once the circle is closed, remove the brooms to their place of storage.

Working with Sumac

Sumac is easy to work with and can present with wonderful colors, such as auburn and plum purple. It is quite soft, so it does require gentle sanding to prevent fuzziness. Do not use sumac for brooms that will take a lot of abuse.

Supplejack

Order: Rosales
Family: Rhamnaceae
Genus: *Berchemia*
Species: *scandens*
Energy: Masculine
Frequency: 12
Element: Fire
Gods: Asgaya Gigagei, Enumclaw
Goddess: Kananeski Anayehi
Properties: Defense, dark energy

Like its much darker cousin the poison ivy, although not related, supplejack is a vascular vine and sturdy when cut or harvested late in maturity. And similar to poison ivy, it is somewhat toxic to humans.

In the Magical Circle: Defense

As with the other dark-energy woods, the supplejack is ideal for defense of yourself, your family, and your house. And the added benefit of the wood is that it may also do positive energy work if asked nicely. Supplejack is rather a down-to-earth defensive wood that will keep you safe. Just make certain that you keep the wood guarded, because since it is a dark-energy conduit, it cannot be responsible for what it may or may not do if given the chance.

Supplejack in circle works positively or negatively. You just have to make certain as you open circle that you state clearly and concisely what it is you wish to accomplish and how the broom may assist you. It does you no good to say something like, "I want to be rich" or "I want to get revenge on whomever." The broom may allow you to be struck by a rich drunk driver, sent to a wheelchair, and given a million dollars. Or it may strike both you and the one you are wanting revenge against by lightning, killing you both. When stating your intent, be articulate, clear, and precise.

Working with Supplejack

Supplejack can not only grow in some beautiful, twisty ways, but it is quite hard when dry and makes an excellent, hardy broomstick. It has a relatively smooth bark, so preparation can vary from full sanding and removal to leaving it intact and natural. This is one of Chelsea's favorite broom materials, and she does some amazing work with the intricacies of the patterns.

Sweetgum

Order: Saxifragales
Family: Altingiaceae
Genus: *Liquidambar*
Species: *styraciflua*
Energy: Masculine
Frequency: 30
Element: Fire
God: Winalagalis
Goddess: Qamaits
Property: Home healing

Sweetgum is another tree that is being banned by city planners and park officials, this time for the seedpods, which when run through a mower become projectiles. Positively, the tree is a good home for beneficial caterpillars when planted in groves away from human populations.

Aside from any problems, the sweetgum tree itself is quite useful. The sap is collected in the early spring along with, but not mixed with, maple sap. Each has a high natural sugar content, and some farms in New England offer a sweetgum syrup that is at times as good as maple syrup.

Magically, the broom is useful for healing circles or being hung around in homes where individuals are ill with blood or nerve diseases or ailments.

In the Magical Circle: Home Healing

There is no circle or ritual that this tree is specifically adept at. The sweetgum is best utilized in the home where the injured or the illness is found. Hang the broom in close proximity to the patient. As the patient moves throughout the day, move the broom with them. Continue to follow prescribed regimens by medical professionals, and the patient should heal quickly.

Working with Sweetgum

Sweetgum is the bully of the playground. It doesn't like to be worked and will fight you every inch of the way. It's a very pitchy tree, which makes it even harder to work in the early spring. It's also very knotty and, therefore, will have interesting markings where the smaller branches were attached. This gives the wood an attractive appearance once you get past the initial woodworking.

Sycamore

Order: Proteales
Family: Platanaceae
Genus: *Platanus*
Species: *occidentalis*
Energy: Feminine
Frequency: 65
Elements: Air, water
God: Osiris
Goddesses: Hathor, Isis, Nut, Kananeski Anayehi
Property: Divination

There is a legend of the introduction of fire to the Cherokee. The Great Spirit placed fire in the hollow of a sycamore and surrounded it by water. No animal could span the water and recover the fire until a spider spun its web to the tree. Placing the fire in a bowl, the spider carried the fire to land on its back. The animals had fire and the spider had the red fire mark on its back.[35]

Sycamore is a wonderful tree to plant around your yard because the bark comes off in sheets and gives an interesting appearance in sun- or moonlight. Further, it is easy enough to find in nurseries and is available anywhere in the country.

In the Magical Circle: Divination

Magically, the sycamore excels in divination. A broom of sycamore will sweep the mist past the veil to expose what is beyond. To do that, procure four sycamore brooms. Place three to form three sides of a square. Light a

35. James Mooney, "The First Fire," in *Myths of the Cherokee*, Extract from the Nineteenth Annual Report of the Bureau of American Ethnology (Government Printing Office, 1902), https://www.gutenberg.org/files/45634/45634-h/45634-h.htm.

white candle about 6 feet from the open side, sit in the box, and place the fourth broom to close the square. Remember to place all the brooms head to toe, like the batteries we spoke of earlier. Concentrate on the candle flame and seek what you wish. To ensure your safety, make certain the brooms make good contact with each other. This puts your space outside the mist of the veil.

Once you have ascertained what you were looking for, thank any deity that assisted you and open the square with the same broom you closed it with. Then blow out the candle and your divination is completed.

Working with Sycamore

Sycamore acts like a conifer it's so soft, but it's also hardy when it dries. Since it's so soft and pliable, great care must be taken to work with it. Work slowly and deliberately, lest you gouge the wood and have to either start over or recalculate your design. We both think you will be pleased with the outcome of a sycamore broom.

Tulip Tree

Order: Magnoliales
Family: Magnoliaceae
Genus: *Liriodendron*
Species: *tulipifera*
Energy: Feminine
Frequency: 49
Element: Water
Gods: Chiron, Paean
Goddesses: Artemis, Hygieia
Property: Working with the underworld

The tulip tree is often mistaken for aspen or poplar until you look at its leaf structure, which is different. The tree is easy to identify by the heart-shaped leaves that are often 4–6 inches across. The tree grows quickly, but if you find it in an open field, you will think that the tree is actually a shrub. Sun stimulates the growth of the tree; however, even in a forest or wooded environment, it will grow to full height and rival other species.

In the Magical Circle: The Underworld

With a tulip tree broom, you can clear a path to the underworld. Be cautious of that, though, and treat that ritual with great care. Do not fail to leave yourself a way back. Toward the end of the incantation to the underworld, make certain you state that you are a visitor to that realm and that while you enjoy visiting, you do not wish to be a permanent resident of the underworld. When it is time to conclude, thank the gods that you met there and then thank them for allowing you to visit, and then leave.

The tulip tree is very similar to poplar. It mimics poplar in all aspects of magical usage and workability. It will do anything you ask of it and therefore respond to whatever you attempt to do to it in the shop. It wants to please and will do whatever you ask. Just be specific. The tree has a tendency to interpret requests out of context.

If you choose to make a tulip tree broom, look at the section on poplar for more magical suggestions.

Working with the Tulip Tree

The tulip tree is a nice wood to work with. It's not too hard, not too soft, not too grainy and not too clean. It works moderately well with hand tools and moderately well with power tools. You may work it during the day or at night. There is no better moon cycle to work it. If this sounds like a commercial for a middle-of-the-road wood, then you are absolutely correct.

Willow

Order: Malpighiales
Family: Salicaceae
Genus: *Salix*
Species: *alba*
Energy: Feminine
Frequency: 98
Elements: Fire, water
Gods: Loki, Poseidon, Zeus
Goddesses: Artemis, Athena, Brigid, Ceridwen, Hel, the Morrigan, Ishtar
Properties: Health, healing

This bark has been ground for hundreds of years as a medicinal cure for headaches due to the high concentration of salicin. The salicin what acetylsalicylic acid is derived from, and that's your active ingredient in most aspirins.

In the Magical Circle: Healing

Willow is the second most powerful of the positive magic woods available to the user. The wood is clear and strong, and once the broom is completed, you will feel the energy coursing through it. This is a go-to wood for healing rituals, and a broom of willow will never let you down as long as you treat it with the respect it deserves. When not in circle, hang it in a place of reverence so that it may protect your house and home.

Willow brooms are excellent for health and healing rituals. If you sweep well a room or area where the occupant is ill or ailing, the positive energies will assist in the healing or comfort of the individual. In circle, use the broom as a wand or athame. Cast as you would normally according to your tradition and use the broom as a conduit between the healing energy of the broom and the individual or individuals who are ill.

Working with Willow

Willow is a joy to work with. The clear white wood responds excellently to sharp tools and a steady hand, and if you are so inclined to try carving the wood, it will respond positively to that also. There is no downside to working with willow.

Wisteria

Order: Fabales
Family: Fabaceae
Genus: *Wisteria*
Species: *frutescens*
Energy: Feminine
Frequency: 59
Element: Air
Gods: A'as, Ganesha, Prometheus
Goddess: Mary
Properties: Clarity, learning

Wisteria wood is readily available as either a rather thin but sturdy and lightweight vine, or when you find a very old plant, the stalk by the ground may be up to a foot in diameter. It is available nationwide as a flower vine spread over fences. The blossoms and flowers are a haven for bees. Even in harsh winter climates, the vines will die back and return in the spring.

In the Magical Circle: Clarity

Magically, a wisteria broom will give you clarity and the ability to learn better than any other broom or wood in the pantheon of vascular plants. After the circle has been cast, take the broom from the altar and use it as a directional tool. Keeping the bristles away from the flame, light a white candle and quietly and calmly stare past the bristles into the fire. The distance is up to you and the space you have to work with, but remember, fire jumps and broom bristles are dry.

Working with Wisteria

For a broom or a whisk, the thicker stalk is preferred, but you may soak and then weave the smaller vines into a sturdy handle for a full-sized broom. Wisteria is a very light and soft wood. We liken it to balsa wood in its weight, but it is much stronger than balsa to work with. However, you must still be careful not to put too much force into the tool that you are working with because the wood will break or gouge if forced to do so.

Witch Hazel

Order: Saxifragales
Family: Hamamelidaceae
Genus: *Hamamelis*
Species: *virginiana*
Energy: Feminine
Frequency: 91
Element: Fire
God: Wong Tai Sin
Goddesses: Sekhmet, Serket, Ta-Bitjet
Properties: Cleaning residual energies, healing

Witch hazel was a staple in our bathrooms growing up. Older individuals will remember having that minty-smelling bottle of witch hazel for sore muscles and pulled tendons in the medicine cabinet. The smell of the plant will bring back those memories.

The plant is usually found as a shrub throughout the country. Its leaves and flowers give a colorful addition to a yard or garden. If you don't prune the living life out of it as most do, then you will get a stately tree with the same attraction as the shrub but with larger branches that will make amazing-smelling broom handles.

In the Magical Circle: Healing

In circle, the witch hazel is used to clean lingering energies and negative influences. Before any important ritual, sweep the circle with a witch hazel broom from south, walking forward clockwise and sweeping outward. Once back at south, back up counterclockwise and sweep again around the circle. This will give you a grounded and neutral space to work with.

Working with Witch Hazel

The bark is soft and comes off easily when green, and the sap keeps the tree green longer than most woods. If you plan on sealing the wood, then you will wait a long time. And if you don't seal the wood, then the sap will get on you and you'll smell as though you just had a rubdown by a Swedish masseuse.

Yew

Order: Pinales
Family: Taxaceae
Genus: *Taxus*
Species: *baccata*
Energies: Masculine and feminine
Frequency: 94
Elements: Air, fire, water
Gods: Hermes, Loki, Odin
Goddesses: Hecate, Hel
Property: Protection

You can't get much more historically English than the yew. The English archers were ruthless with their yew bows and cut the French to ribbons at the Battle of Agincourt. If you are looking for a broom with attitude, then yew is it. Yew knows it's important. It knows it was one of the sacred woods of the Druids.

In the Magical Circle: Protection

Magically, the yew is best used for protection. We have talked about poison ivy and padauk being good for protection and aggression with a dark side, but yew won't have any of that. Yew is all light energy but can be snarky in that regard. If you are asking it to protect you from something, the yew may make the determination that you don't need protecting at all. So in circle or in your home, if you use a yew, be kind to it, treat it with reverence, and ask nicely if you want something.

Working with Yew

Yew is easy to work with. It tools easily. The wood is soft, and if you use a lathe, the pieces are long and aromatic. Yew ends up with a yellowish wood that turns light to medium orange as it ages.

However, Yew is another tree that is poisonous to both humans and animals, so be careful when working with it. Wear protective equipment and wash thoroughly when finished.

SECTION 3: Broom Recipes

Brooms can be almost any shape or form, from the simple and utilitarian to the impractical and artistic or a combination of both. Part of the fun of this craft is playing around with techniques and materials to come up with combinations that appeal to you.

Each of the following recipes teaches a different technique or techniques somewhere in it, but the majority will be very similar between broom styles. We have done this to expose you to some of the design possibilities that you can then mix and match as you see fit and even come up with creative ideas of your own.

There are six types of brooms listed in this section: the cobwebber, the hearth broom, two types of kitchen brooms, a turkey wing whisk, and a hawk tail whisk, but don't let that restrict you. You can make brooms any size or shape that you like!

COBWEBBER

This is a perfect beginner broom due to its simplicity and one that comes in incredibly handy around the house. It is long and slender so that all the cobwebs and dust in the corners of the ceiling can get swept away. Its size and shape also make it an excellent ritual broom, as it is not cumbersome or heavy to use. For this broom, we will be weaving the stems of craft broomcorn.

Materials

- 1 stick for handle: ¾–1 inch in diameter and 1–4 feet long
- 12 stalks outer broomcorn, even in length from knuckle to end of hurl
- #18 nylon twine
- 6- or 7-ply waxed linen thread
- Jerk string

Directions

Soak the stems of the broomcorn by filling a five-gallon bucket with water deep enough to submerge the stem end, knuckle, and about 3 inches of hurl of the broomcorn. Soak for at least thirty minutes. After soaking, remove broomcorn from water, drain for two minutes, and set somewhere close to you.

Prepare your workspace and wind your spinner with approximately 15 feet of nylon twine. Thread the twine through the bottom hole of your stick and tie. Wrap the twine around the stick tightly three times, with the twine going over the top of the stick and away from you.

Put one stem of broomcorn under the twine and against the stick, with the hurl to your left and the twine about ½ inch above the knuckle. Turn the stick toward you so that the stalk is trapped between the stick and twine.

Place another stem next to the first one in the same way without overlapping the stems. Pull tight enough so that the twine makes an indentation in the stem of the broomcorn and continue to keep tension tight.

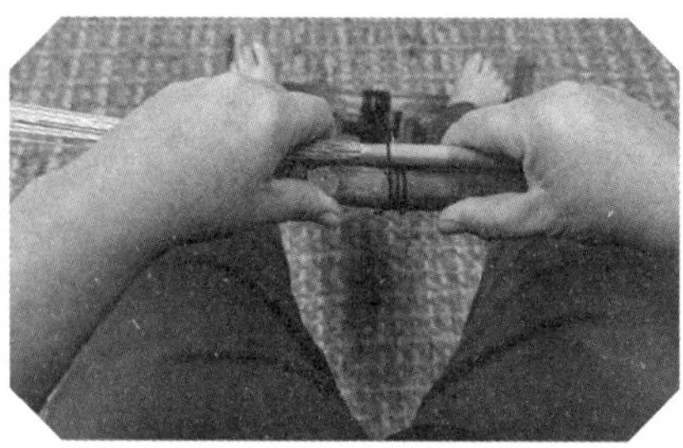

Image #27: Putting broomcorn under the twine

Continue putting stems of broomcorn around the stick so that they are tightly against each other but not overlapping. Once there are stems of broomcorn completely encircling the stick, wrap them tightly three times, working toward the right. The number of stalks needed will vary, but you want to end up with an odd number so that the weave will properly spiral.

To plait, gently bend down a stalk of broomcorn and slide the twine below it. You may hear some cracking or light breaking, but the stalk should remain whole. If it does not, replace that stalk. The twine then goes over the top of the next stalk. Alternate putting the twine over and under the stalks as you work your way around the broom, moving to the right. The pattern will begin to spiral naturally as you work.

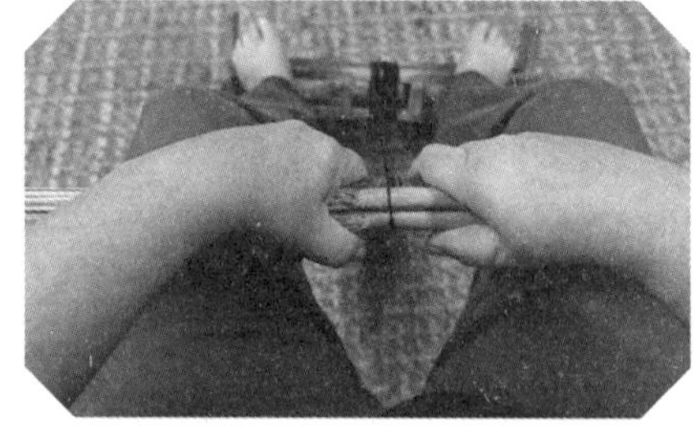

Image #28: Adding the second stem

At the end of the plait, and when the twine is in an over position, fold the jerk string in half and place it under the twine, with the loop to your right toward the top of the stick. Wrap the twine around the broom at least three more times, with the jerk string staying underneath the twine and with the loop exposed from underneath the wraps to the right.

Press the twine tightly against the stems with your left thumbnail just below the jerk string. Use a lighter to cut the twine between the broom and the spinner. Your thumbnail should be holding the wraps tightly so the twine tension is not released.

Thread the melted cut end of the twine through the loop on the jerk string and pull it tightly with your right hand, taking over the tension from the left thumbnail.

Use your left hand to yank the ends of the jerk string so that the threaded loop gets pulled completely below the wraps. Pull as tight as you can.

Use your knife to cut the end of the twine as close as possible to the wraps, locking the twine in place. Refer to the tying off section in chapter 5 for more information.

Trim the stalks to ¼ inch above the top wraps with your knife.

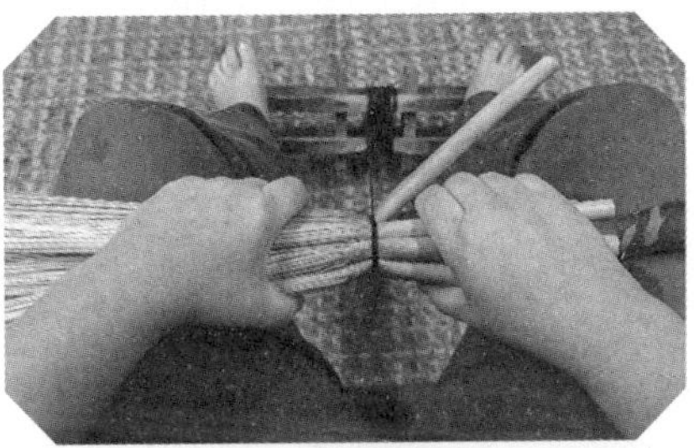

Image #29: Bending the stalk back to plait; Image #30: Plaiting the stalk

Image #31: Trimming the broomcorn

Allow the broom to dry for several days or until the broomcorn under the wraps is dry before continuing to the sewing stage. Use the round broom technique in chapter 5 to stitch the brush into its final shape.

HEARTH BROOM

Just as its name describes, the round hearth broom is the perfect size for sweeping out the hearth, but it is also great for any confined space such as tiny homes, RVs, or even treehouses. It makes a great midsize ritual broom for taking to coven circles and sabbats. On this broom, we'll use a V-up technique to secure the broomcorn to the broom handle quickly and decoratively.

Materials

- 1 stick for handle: ¾–1 inch diameter and up to 30 inches long
- 10 stems inner broomcorn
- 10 stems outer broomcorn
- #18 nylon twine
- 6- or 7-ply waxed linen thread.
- Jerk string

Directions

Use a knife to split the outer broomcorn lengthwise down the stem and brush.

Using a five-gallon bucket, soak the stems of the broomcorn in water deep enough to submerge the stalk, knuckle, and about 3 inches of hurl for at least thirty minutes. After soaking, remove broomcorn from water and set it close to you. Keep the inner and outer piles separate.

Prepare your workspace and wind your spinner with approximately 20 feet of nylon twine. Thread the twine through the bottom hole of your stick and tie. Using both feet on your spinner, one on either side of the twine, hold tension on the twine as you make three wraps around your stick toward the right by spinning the stick toward you. The twine should be going over top of the stick and away from you.

Release more twine as needed by pulling the twine, using your feet to control the spinner. Always keep tension tight. Turn, pull, turn, pull…

Layer 1:

Put one stem of inner broomcorn under the twine and against the stick, with the hurl to your left and the twine about ½ inch above the knuckle. Rotate the stick toward you so that the stem is trapped between the stick and twine.

Place another inner stem next to the first one in the same way without overlapping the stems. Pull tight enough so that the twine makes an indentation in the stem of the broomcorn and always continue keeping tension tight.

Continue putting stems of inner broomcorn around the stick so that they are tightly against each other but not overlapping. Once there are stems of broomcorn completely encircling the stick, wrap the twine around them tightly three times, working toward the right. The number of stems necessary will vary depending on the diameter of your stick and the thickness of the stems.

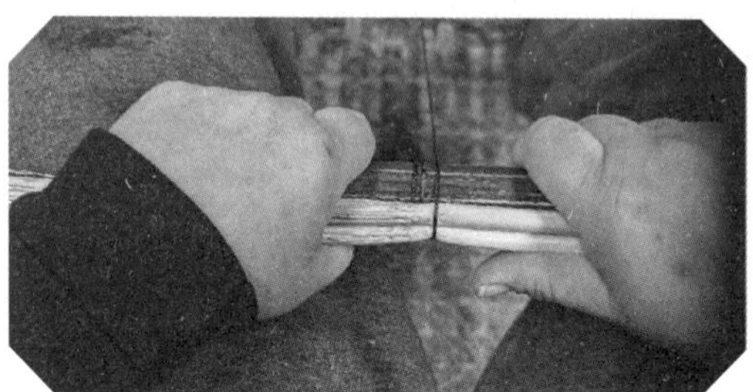

Image #32: Adding stems around the stick

Layer 2:

Begin adding the outer broomcorn halves in a second layer on top of the first one, using the same method as the previous layer. Be sure to put the smooth side out and the cut side in.

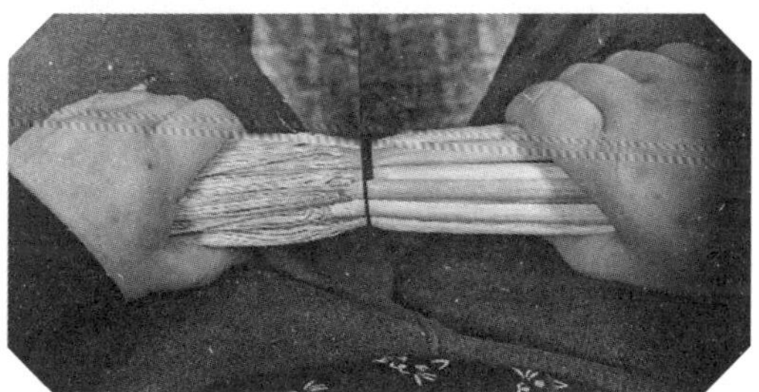

Image #33: Starting the second layer

Once broomcorn completely encircles the broom, wrap tightly three times, working toward the right.

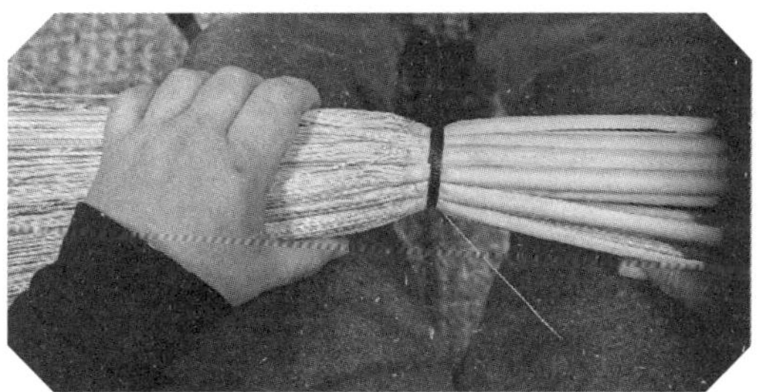

Image #34: Completed second layer

V-up by bringing the twine up 1 inch as you wrap once. Make five wraps above the V-up.

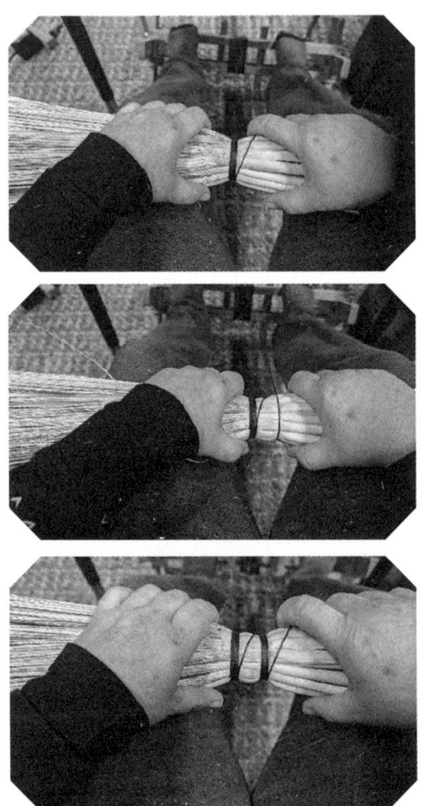

Image #35: Pull the twine up with your index finger; Image #36: Wrap three times; Image #37: Repeat the V-up

Repeat the last step as many times as you like to get the look you want. We usually do three to five V-ups.

After your last V-up, fold the jerk string in half and place it under the twine with the loop to your right toward the top of the stick. Wrap the twine around four more times with the jerk string staying underneath the twine, leaving the loop exposed.

Press the twine tightly against the stems with your left thumbnail. Use a lighter to cut the twine between the broom and the spinner. Your thumbnail should be holding the wraps tightly so the tension on the broom itself is not released.

Thread the melted cut end of the twine through the loop on the jerk string and pull it tightly with your right hand, taking over the tension from the left thumbnail.

Use your left hand to yank the ends of the jerk string so that the threaded loop gets pulled below the wraps. Pull as tight as you can.

Use your knife to cut the end of the twine as close as possible to the wraps, locking the twine in place. Refer to the tying off section in chapter 5 for more information.

Trim the stems to ¼ inch above the top wraps with your knife.

Allow the broom to dry for several days or until the broomcorn under the wraps is dry before continuing to the sewing stage. Use either the round or flat broom technique in chapter 5 to stitch the brush into its final desired shape.

Image #38: Completed V-ups

KITCHEN BROOM with KNURL

This full-size kitchen broom is incredibly effective, working wonderfully for your chores or for dancing around a bonfire. It is made with knurl, which is the full length of craft broomcorn from the stem to the tips of the brush.

Materials

- 1 stick for handle: ¾–1 inches diameter and approximately 42 inches long
- 17 inner stalks of broomcorn
- 23 outer stalks of broomcorn with similar lengths of stalk
- #18 nylon twine
- 6- or 7-ply waxed linen thread
- Jerk string

Directions

Fill a five-gallon bucket and soak the stems of the broomcorn in water deep enough to submerge the stalk, knuckle, and about 3 inches of hurl for at least thirty minutes. After soaking, remove the broomcorn from the water, drain for two minutes, and set somewhere close to you, keeping the inner and outer stems in separate piles.

Prepare your workspace and wind your spinner with approximately 30 feet of nylon twine. Thread the twine through the bottom hole of your stick and tie. Wrap the twine around the stick tightly three times, with the twine going over the top of the stick and away from you and moving toward the right.

Using both feet on your spinner, one on either side of the twine, hold tension on the twine as you make three wraps around your stick by spinning the stick toward you. The twine should be going over top of the stick and away from you. Release more twine as needed by pulling the twine, using your feet to hold and control the spinner. Always keep tension tight. Turn, pull, turn, pull…

Layer 1

Place one stalk of inner broomcorn under the twine and against the stick, with the hurl to your left and the twine about ½ inch above the knuckle. Rotate the stick toward you so that the stalk is trapped between the stem and twine.

Place another inner stalk against the first one in the same way without overlapping stems.

Continue placing stalks of inner broomcorn around the stick so that they are tightly against each other but not overlapping. Pull the twine tight enough so that it makes an indentation in the stem of the broomcorn. Remember to keep the tension tight at all times.

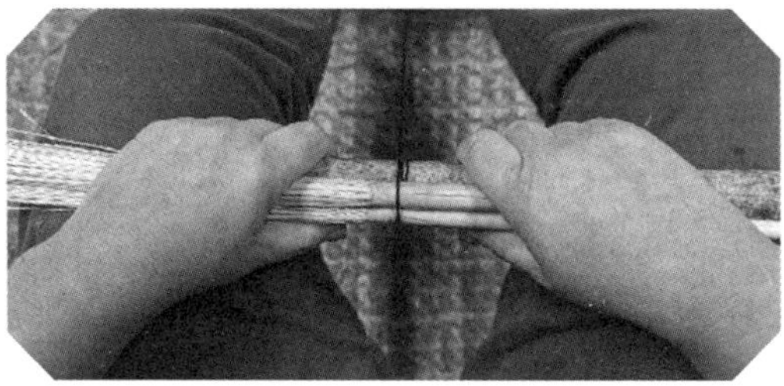

Image #39: Adding stems around the stick

Once broomcorn is completely encircling the stick, wrap three times, moving to the right. The number of stalks needed will vary.

Image #40: Stems completely encircled

Layer 2:

This is the shoulder layer. Rotate broom halfway. Stack three stems of broomcorn in a pyramid shape and place under the twine on one side of the broom, then rotate halfway and pyramid another three stems and place them under the twine on the other side of the broom. This creates shoulders on either side. Wrap three times.

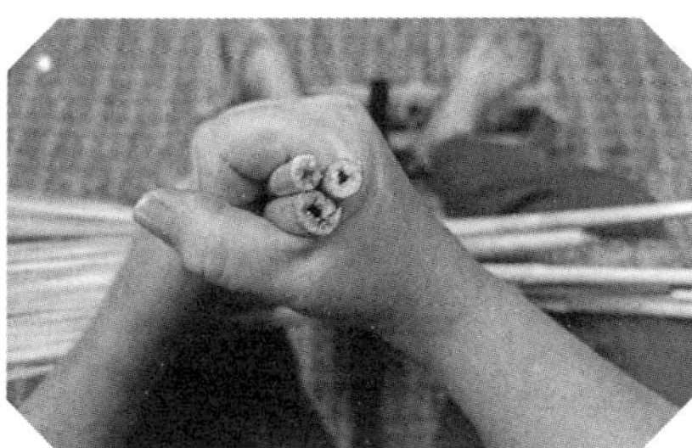

Image #41: Cluster of three stems;
Image #42: Adding clusters to opposite sides

Use your knife to cut the stems of the broomcorn to a taper against the stick. You will see an oval shape form when looking down on the broomcorn from the top of the broom.

Image #43: Trimming the stems to a taper

Layer 3:

Next, we work on the outer layer. Make a layer of outer broomcorn on top of the shouldered one using the same method as layer 1. Keep the tension tight!

Once completely around the broom, wrap three times, working toward the right. End with an odd number of stems so that the plaiting will spiral.

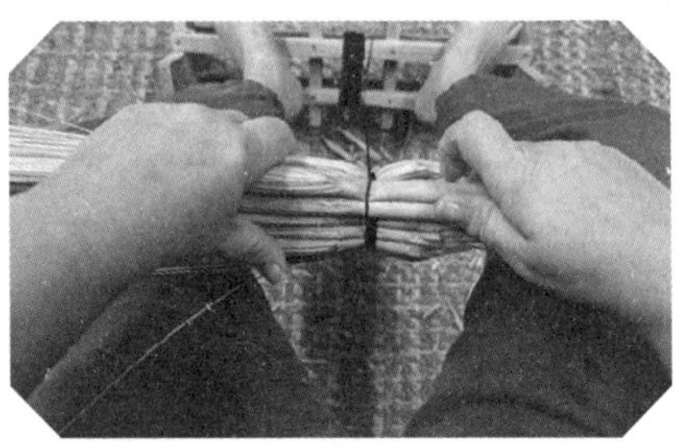

Image #44: Starting the outer layer

To plait, gently bend down a stalk of broomcorn and slide the twine below it. You may hear some cracking or light breaking, but the stalk should remain whole. If it does break or cut through, replace that stalk. The twine then goes over the top of the next stalk. Alternate putting the twine over and under the stalks as you work your way around the broom, moving to the right. The pattern will begin to spiral naturally as you work.

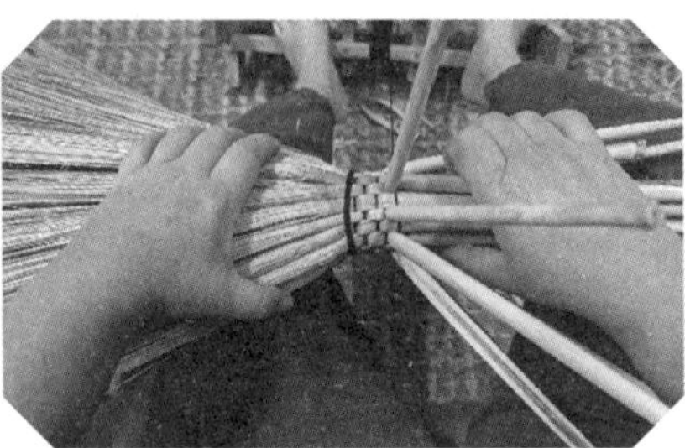

Image #45: Bending the stem to plait; Image #46: Plaiting the stems

When you reach the top of layer three's stems, pinch the stems together against the broom handle. Wrap three times.

Place the jerk string under the twine, with the loop to your right, toward the top of the stick .

Wrap the twine around three more times, with the jerk string staying underneath the twine.

Press the twine tightly against the stalks with your left thumbnail. Use a lighter to "cut" the twine between the broom and the spinner. Your thumbnail should be holding the wraps tightly so the twine tension on the broom itself is not released.

Thread the melted end of the twine through the loop on the jerk string and hold it tightly with your right hand.

Use your left hand to yank the ends of the jerk string so that the threaded loop gets pulled all the way under the wraps. This should be very tight.

Cut the end of the twine as close as possible to the wraps. Refer to the tying off section in chapter 5 for more information.

Use your knife to trim the stalks to about ¼ inch above the top wraps.

Allow the broom to dry thoroughly for several days before continuing to the sewing stage using the flat broom technique (see chapter 5).

KITCHEN BROOM with HURL

We have adapted this method of creating a kitchen broom from a technique by broom maker Shawn Hoefer of Havencroft Farm & Fiber. This method creates a gorgeous, heavy-duty broom with pronounced shoulders that looks more like the modern brooms we are familiar with. This is an advanced broom technique, so we recommend starting with the previous brooms in this chapter.

This kitchen broom is made from hurl, which is just the loose brush separated from the stem and de-seeded. We will weave this broom with a cap made of cut and split broomcorn stems to cover the weave.

Materials

- Approximately 1-inch diameter by 42-inch-length stick for handle
- 20 ounces (5 4-ounce bundles) of broomcorn hurl
- 8 7-inch lengths of equally thick stems cut from craft broomcorn (Stems can also be purchased separately.)
- #18 nylon twine or 6- or 7-ply waxed linen thread
- Jerk string
- Velcro

Directions

Split each stem into quarters lengthwise. Remove a small portion of the pith on the inside of the stalks to prevent them from becoming waterlogged and splitting while weaving. Soak them completely submerged in water for at least one hour. Hot water will make the process go faster.

Fill a five-gallon bucket with water deep enough to submerge the bottom third of the hurl, and allow to soak for at least ten minutes. After soaking, remove the broomcorn from the water and drain for two minutes.

Divide the soaked broomcorn into bunches by splitting two of the bundles into three parts each and the remaining three bundles into halves. You should now have a total of twelve bunches. Stack the bunches in a crisscross pattern with the six smaller bundles on the top of the stack.

Prepare your workspace and wind your spinner with approximately 30 feet of nylon twine. Thread the twine through the bottom hole of your stick and tie. Using both feet on your spinner, one on either side of the twine, hold tension on the twine as you make three wraps around your stick and over the tail of the twine, working toward the left, by spinning the stick toward you. The twine should be going over top of the stick and away from you. Release more twine as needed by pulling the twine, using your feet to control the spinner. Always keep tension tight. Turn, pull, turn, pull…

Layer 1:

Starting from the top of the stack, place one bunch under the twine and against the stick with approximately 1 inch of hurl to the right of the twine and the remaining to the left. Rotate the stick one-quarter turn toward you.

Place another bunch of hurl next to the previous bunch without overlapping. Rotate stick one-quarter turn toward you.

Image #47: Adding bunches to stick

Repeat for two more bunches. You should now have a total of four bunches equally distributed around the stick. Make three tight wraps, working toward the right. Looking down from the top of the stick; you should see hurl completely and evenly encircling the stick.

Layer 2:

Place one bunch under the twine on one side of the previous layer without distributing it, creating a shoulder. Rotate the stick one-half turn toward you.

Place another bunch on the opposite side of the previous one. Rotate stick one-half turn. You should now have small shoulders on your broom, creating an oval shape when viewed from the top of the stick. Make three more tight wraps toward the right

Layer 3:

Now, you should be on to the bigger bunches in your stack. Place one bunch over top of one of the shoulders *upside down*. You should have approximately 1½ inches of the stem end of the hurl to the *left* of the twine and the remaining brush end pointing to the right.

Image #48: Upside down shoulders

Rotate stick one-half turn. Repeat the last step for the second shoulder. Make three more tight wraps.

Gently bend the long ends of the hurl down toward the bottom of the broom, which will give the brooms its pronounced shoulders. Use a Velcro strap to gently but tightly tie all of the brush together to keep it tidy and easier to work with.

Image #49: Bending over the shoulders

Layer 4:

Spiral the twine up over the top of the hurl and make three more tight wraps directly against the stick.

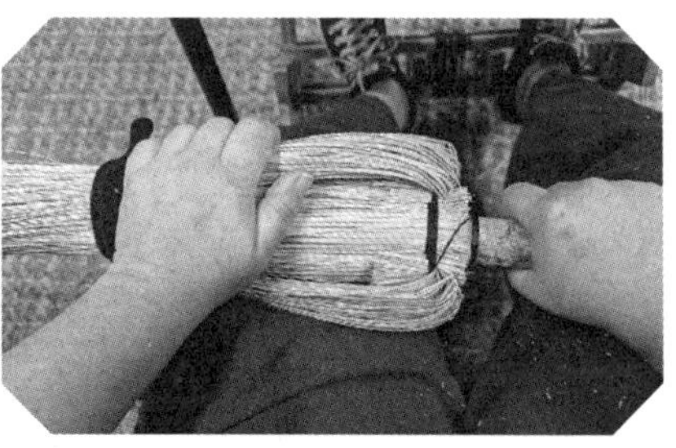

Image #50: Bringing twine above the hurl

This is where things get difficult. Remove the next two bundles from the stack and divide them in half. Bend the top of one bunch approximately 2 inches from the stem end, creating a crease in the bunch. Place the bend of the bunch under the twine with the brush end to your left and the stem end to your right, distributing it evenly around one quarter of the stick. The bend should be right where the stick and the previous layers meet. The long brush end of the hurl will splay out sideways.

Image #51: Adding the outer layers

Up until now, the twine has always been moving up the stick. Now, force the twine down toward the brush end to prevent the broomcorn from sliding up the handle. Add the remaining three divided bunches and distribute evenly around the stick and wrap three to five times toward the *left*.

Image #52: Finished outer layers

Layer 5:

Repeat layer 4. Remove the inner Velcro strap and use it to gently pull all of the brush together so it is no longer splaying out sideways. Trim the top of the hurl to about 2 inches above your last wraps.

Begin placing cut and soaked stems shiny side down under the twine with about ¾ inch of the stem to the right of the twine and the remainder to the left until you have completely encircled the hurl. Keep them tightly together but not overlapping. End with an odd number of stems. Wrap five times toward your *left*.

Image #53: Cut and soaked stems added

Now, we will begin working up the broom again toward the right. Circle up ½ inch and wrap three times.

Fold the left side of the stems over the twine toward the right. When you have gone all the way around, the twine will come out over the stems ½ inch up from the fold. Wrap three more times.

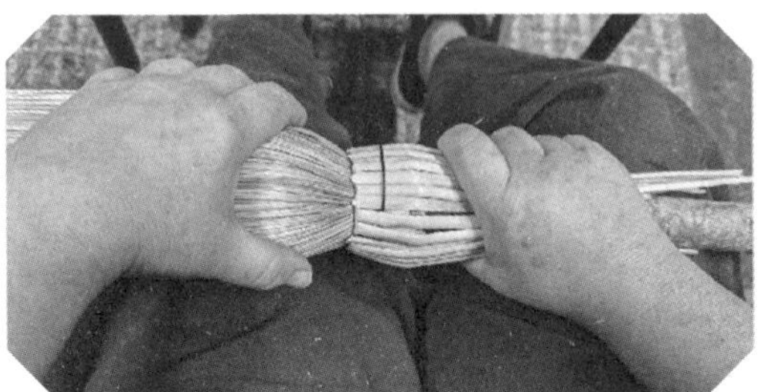

Image #54: Stems folded upward

To plait, gently fold a stem to the left and bring the twine beneath it. The twine then goes over the next stem. Repeat this process of weaving the twine over and under successive stems, continuing around the broom. The pattern will begin to spiral naturally.

Image #55: Beginning plaiting

Just before you get to the top of the hurl, wrap three times.

Rotate the stick halfway while bringing the twine up above the hurl. Pinch the tops of the stems tightly against the stick and wrap tightly three times. If you would like to and there is plenty of the split stalk remaining against the handle, attempt to align them so that only one layer is visible on the surface and continue to weave until approximately 1 inch of stalk remains.

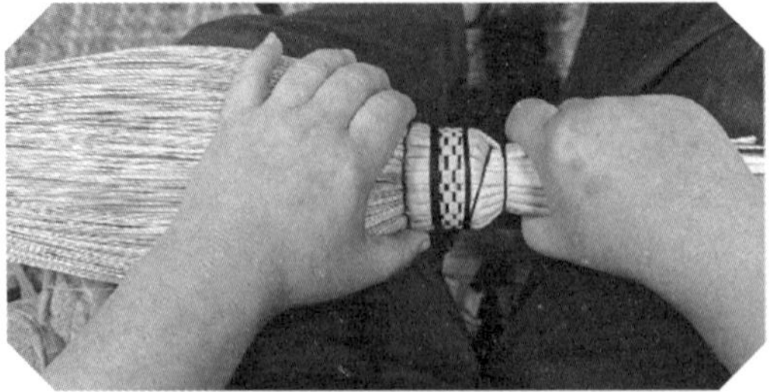

Image #56: Pinched stems

Fold the jerk string in half and place it under the twine with the loop to your right toward the top of the stick. Wrap the twine around three more times, with the jerk string staying underneath the twine and leaving the loop exposed.

Press the twine tightly against the stems with your left thumbnail. Use a lighter to cut the twine between the broom and the spinner. Your thumbnail should be holding the wraps tightly so the tension on the broom itself is not released.

Thread the melted cut end of the twine through the loop on the jerk string and pull it tightly with your right hand, taking over the tension from the left thumbnail.

Use your left hand to yank the ends of the jerk string so that the threaded loop gets pulled below the wraps. Pull as tight as you can, locking the twine in place.

Use your knife to cut the end of the twine as close as possible to the wraps. Refer to the tying off section in chapter 5 for more information.

Trim the stems to ¼ inch above the top wraps with your knife.

Allow the broom to dry for several days or until the broomcorn under the wraps is dry before continuing to the sewing stage. Use the flat broom technique to stitch the brush into its final shape (see chapter 5).

TURKEY WING WHISK

It is rumored within the broom making community that before broomcorn whisks were invented, people would use an actual turkey wing, which this whisk resembles, to clean up small messes. This useful whisk is simple to make using a technique called a V-up instead of weaving. It can be made in many different sizes and is perfect for the altar due to its lightness and compact size. Stitching this broom is optional.

Materials

- 6 ounces hurl (1½ 4-ounce bundles)
- #18 nylon twine
- 6- or 7-ply waxed linen thread (optional)
- Jerk string
- Hanging cord

Directions

Prepare your workspace and wind your spinner with approximately 30 feet of nylon twine.

Divide the 6-ounce bundle into eight equal bunches by dividing in half, half again, and then divide *three* of those bunches in half again. You now have seven bundles, with one bundle being twice the size of the remaining six. Crisscross the bunches into a single stack with the double bundle on top, and place within easy reach.

Hold the top (double) bunch in your right hand with the wispy ends of the hurl to your left. Bring the twine over top of the spinner and toward you. Hold the end of the twine against the hurl of the top bunch approximately 6 inches from the wispy ends.

Using both feet on your spinner, one on either side of the twine, hold tension on the twine as you make three wraps around the bunch and over the end of the twine by rotating the spinner toward you. The twine should be going over top of the hurl and away from you toward the right. Release more twine as needed by pulling the twine, using your feet to control the spinner. Always keep tension tight. Turn, pull, turn, pull…

Image #57: Wrapping the first bundle

Place a single bunch from your stack against the first bunch, hiding the tail of the twine between the bunches. Wrap twice, keeping the added bunch on one side and not distributed around the previous bunch.

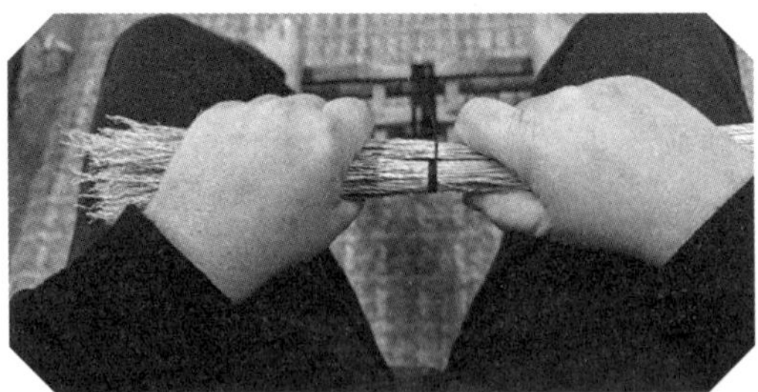

Image #58: Adding the next bundle

V-up one wrap around the combined bundle by bringing the twine up 1 inch as you wrap once. Make three wraps above the V-up.

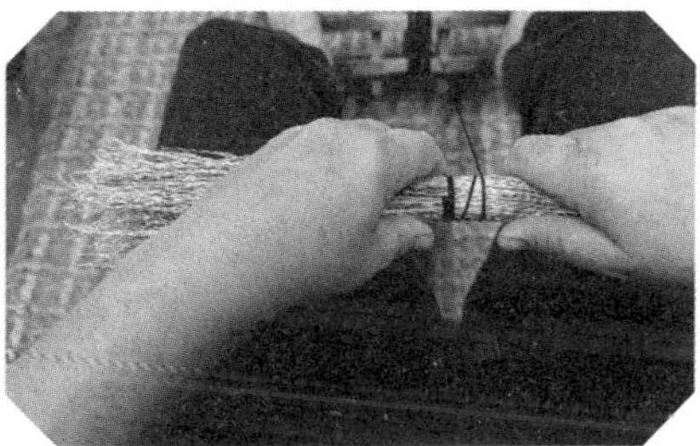

Image #59 & 60: Creating the V-up

Add another bunch on the same side as the previous bunch under the twine against the combined bundle. Wrap and V-up as before.

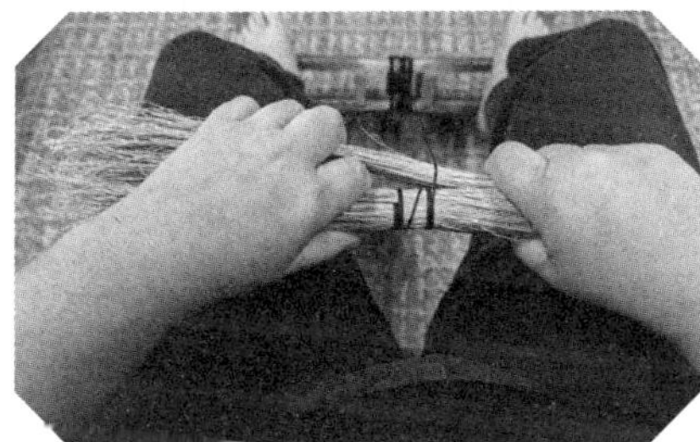
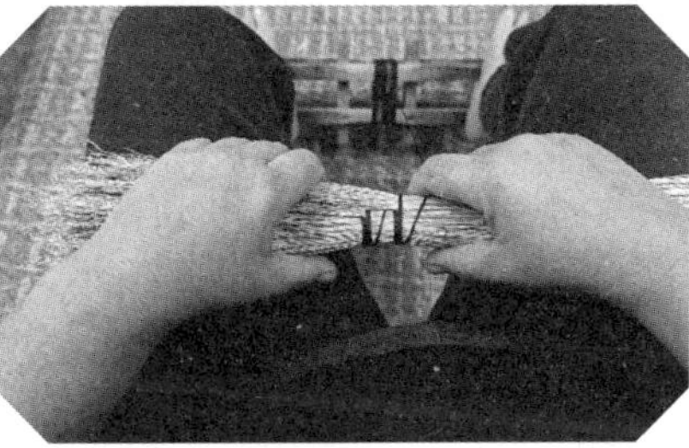

Image #61: Add another bundle; Image #62: V-up

Continue adding bunches on the same side until you are through the pile. One side of your whisk should show V-ups and the other should show straight lines.

Image #63: All bundles attached

After all bundles are attached, continue wrapping up the hurl using V-ups, creating a handle. Just before the end of the whisk, fold your hanging loop in half and insert it under the twine with the loop to the right. Wrap once.

Fold the jerk string in half and place it under the twine, with the loop to your right toward the top of the handle. Wrap the twine around the whisk three more times with the jerk string staying underneath the twine and with the loop exposed from underneath the wraps to the right.

Image #64: Continue wrapping up the handle

Press the twine tightly against the handle with your left thumbnail just below the jerk string. Use a lighter to cut the twine between the broom and the spinner. Your thumbnail should be holding the wraps tightly so the twine tension is not released.

Thread the melted cut end of the twine through the loop on the jerk string and pull it tightly with your right hand, taking over the tension from the left thumbnail.

Use your left hand to yank the ends of the jerk string so that the threaded loop gets pulled all the way under the wraps. Pull as tight as you can.

Use your knife to cut the end of the twine as close as possible to the wraps, locking the twine in place. Refer to the tying off section in chapter 5 for more information.

Trim the end of the hurl to about ¼ inch above the top wraps.

Image #65: Trimmed end of whisk

If stitching is desired, continue to the sewing stage using the flat broom technique (see chapter 5).

HAWK TAIL WHISK

With bunches of broomcorn added to both sides, the hawk tail is a balanced whisk that can be used at the altar or to dust your house. In fact, we think it makes a great car broom since it is compact and easy to tuck away in a door pocket or trunk! This recipe uses basket reed for a decorative addition to the weave. Note that you do not need to stitch this broom.

Materials

- 6 ounces hurl (1½ 4-ounce bundles)
- 25 7-inch pieces of ¼-inch flat or flat-oval basket reed, soaked at least ten minutes
- #18 nylon twine
- 6- or 7-ply waxed linen thread (optional)
- Hanging cord
- Jerk string

Directions

Fill a five-gallon bucket with water deep enough to submerge the bottom half of the hurl for ten minutes. After soaking, remove the hurl from water and drain for two minutes. Divide bundle into 12 equal bunches by dividing in half, then half again, and then thirds. Combine two of the bunches, so you now have 11 bunches. Crisscross the bundles into one stack with the double bunch on top and place within easy reach.

Prepare your workspace and wind your spinner with approximately 15 feet of nylon twine. Bring twine over top of the spinner and toward you.

Hold the top (double) bunch in your right hand with the wispy ends of the hurl to your left. Bring the twine over top of the spinner and toward you. Hold the end of the twine against the hurl approximately 6 inches from the wispy ends.

Using both feet on your spinner, one on either side of the twine, hold tension on the twine as you make three wraps around the bunch and over the end of the twine by rotating the spinner toward you. The twine should be going over top of the hurl and away from you toward the right. Release more twine as needed by pulling the twine, using your feet to control the spinner. Always keep tension tight. Turn, pull, turn, pull...

Image #66: Starting the first bunch

Place a single bunch against the first bunch, hiding the tail of the twine. Wrap once, keeping the bunch on one side, not distributed around the previous bunch.

Image #67: Adding the second bunch

Turn the whisk halfway and place another bundle directly opposite the previous bundle. Wrap two times.

Image #68: Adding the third bunch to the opposite side

V-up one wrap around the combined bundle by bringing the twine up 1 inch while wrapping. Wrap three times.

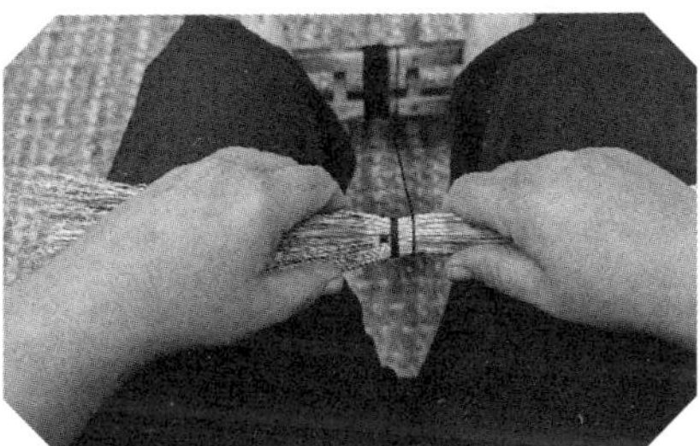

Image #69: V-up; Image #70: Wrap three times

Add one bunch to the same side as your first bunch. Turn the whisk halfway and add another bunch to the same side as your second bunch. Wrap two times.

V-up one wrap around the combined handle. Wrap three times.

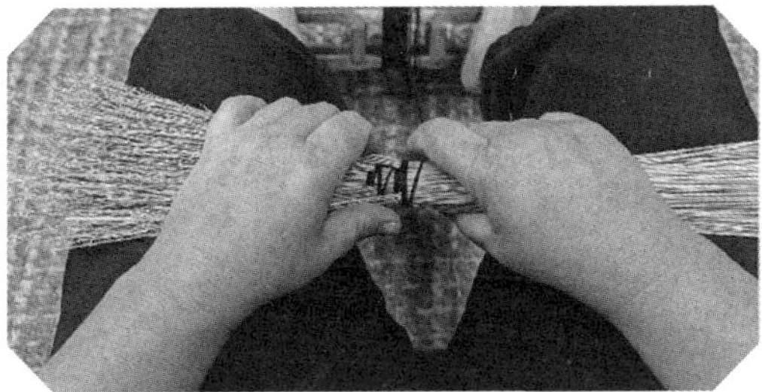

Image #71: Adding bunches to each side

Continue adding bunches as before until you have five bunches on each side. The front should show V-ups, and the back should show only straight lines.

After all bundles are attached, tightly spiral up the hurl, creating a handle. Wrap three times.

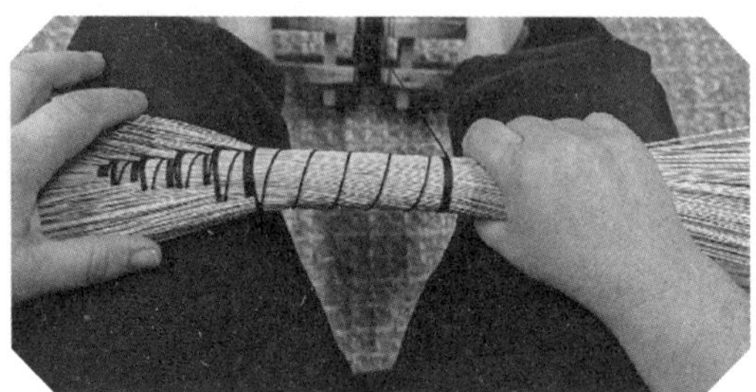

Image #72: Spiral up the handle

Begin placing soaked and cut basket reed under the twine with 6 inches of reed to the *right* and about 1 inch tucked beneath the twine to the left. Keep them tightly together but not overlapping until you have completely encircled the handle. End with an odd number of reeds so that it will weave properly.

Image #73: Adding reed to the handle

Wrap three times. Spiral down ½ inch and wrap three more times.

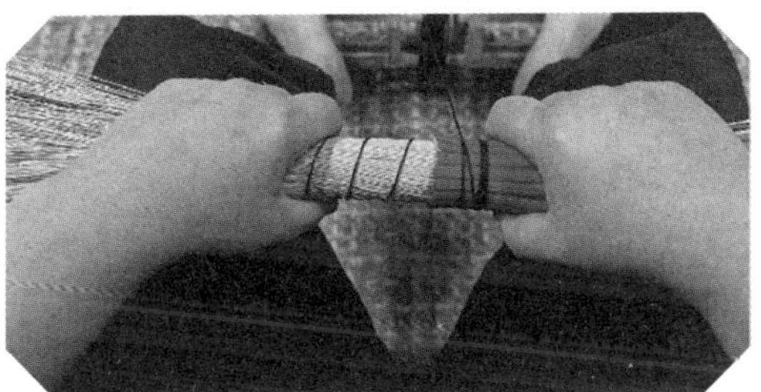

Image #74: Spiral down ½ inch

Fold the long ends of the reed to the left over the twine. The twine will come out from underneath when all of the reeds have been folded over. Wrap three more times.

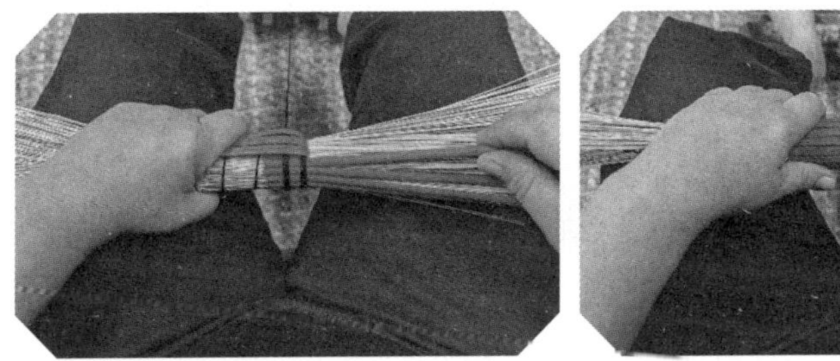

Image #75: Fold reed over; Image #76: Wrap around reed

To plait, gently bend a single piece of reed toward the right and slide the twine below it. You may hear some cracking or breaking, but the reed should remain whole. If it does not, replace that reed. The twine then goes over the top of the next reed. Alternate over and under the reeds as you work your way around the broom, moving to the right. The pattern will begin to spiral naturally as you work.

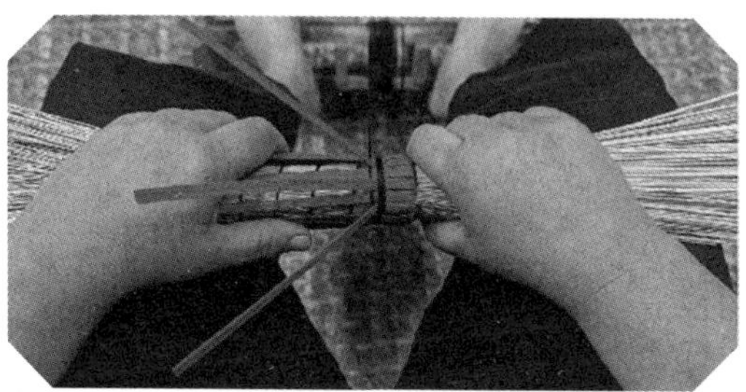

Image #77: Plaiting the reed

When you reach the flare of the whisk, wrap one time. Fold the jerk string in half and place it under the twine, with the loop to your right toward the bottom of the broom. Wrap the twine around the plait three more times, with the jerk string staying underneath the twine and with the loop exposed from underneath the wraps to the right.

Press the twine tightly against the reed with your left thumbnail. Use a lighter to "cut" the twine between the broom and the spinner. Your thumbnail should be holding the wraps tightly so the tension on the broom itself is not released.

Thread the melted cut end of the twine through the loop on the jerk string and hold it tightly with your left hand.

Use your right hand to yank the ends of the jerk string so that the threaded loop gets pulled below the wraps. This should be very tight. Cut the end of the twine as close as possible to the wraps so that you can no longer see the end of the twine. Refer to the tying off section in chapter 5 for more information.

Trim the reed to about ¼ inch below the final wraps of the handle.

Trim the hurl to about ¼ inch above the top of the woven stalks.

If stitching is desired, allow the broom to dry for several days or until the hurl and reed are dry before continuing to the flat sewing stage (see chapter 5).

Conclusion

Brooms are essential, and once you begin your journey down that long and very entertaining rabbit hole, you will come out the other end a better craftsperson and, we shall expect, a better magic user. As we said earlier, use this book as a grimoire for your brooms. Write in this book. Draw pictures. Use arrows and whatever language you use to articulate what you need to remember. This is your book, and like your broom, if you leave it on the shelf and admire how pretty the spine is, it will eventually stop helping you.

We have faith in you. You cared enough about your magical tools to purchase, borrow, or covertly read this book, and for that we applaud you. Be good to the earth, the Craft, and your fellows. They deserve nothing less.

Appendix A
Woods by Deities

A

A'as: Wisteria
Ala: Padauk
Alaunus: Hemlock
Ame-no-Koyane: Golden rain tree
Ame-no-Uzume: Golden rain tree
Amaethon: Black locust
Amaterasu: Olive
Anyanwu: Padauk
Aphrodite: Black walnut, crepe myrtle, pear, rosemary, rowan
Apollo: Hickory, laurel, olive
Arduinna: Hornbeam
Ares: Holly
Artemis: Black walnut, cherry, chestnut, crepe myrtle, Douglas fir, mimosa, oak, tulip tree, willow
Asgaya Gigagei: Supplejack
Asintmah: Hickory
Astarte: Black walnut, crepe myrtle, pine
Athena: Maple, olive, willow

B

Bacchus: Douglas fir
Baldur: Eastern red cedar, laurel

Brahma: Privet
Bran: Alder
Brigid: Hawthorn, oak, rowan, willow

C

Ceres: Laurel
Ceridwen: Beech, black locust, elm, oak, rowan, spruce, willow
Cernunnos: Oak, pear
Chantico: Sumac
Cihuacoatl: Sumac
Chiron: Tulip tree
Cronus: Dogwood
Cupid: Orange
Cybele: Spruce

D

Danu: Holly
Dian Cécht: Hemlock
Diana: Apple, black walnut, chestnut, douglas fir, oak
Dionysus: Elm, fig

E

Enumclaw: Supplejack
Erebus: Datura

F

Fei Lian: Mulberry
Freya: Alder, birch
Freyr: Elder, holly, magnolia
Frigg: Ash, hawthorn
Fujin: Mulberry

G

Gaia: Dogwood, elder, elm, holly
Ganesha: Wisteria
Guanyin: Gingko

H

Hathor: Crepe myrtle, sycamore
Hebe: Rowan
Hecate: Black locust, cottonwood, datura, hemlock, poplar, rowan, yew
Hel: Beech, black walnut, eastern red cedar, datura, elder, elm, poison ivy, willow, yew
Hera: Pear
Hercules: Olive
Hermaphroditus: Elm, persimmon
Hermes: Yew
Herne: Oak
Horus: Olive
Huehueteotl: Sumac
Hygieia: Tulip tree
Hypnos: Datura

I

Indra: Datura
Isis: Douglas fir, fig, sycamore
Ishtar: Willow
Ixchel: Hackberry

J

Jord: Magnolia
Juno: Fig
Jupiter: Fig, maple

K

Kali: Datura
Kananeski Anayehi: Supplejack, sycamore
Kichijoten: Mulberry
Kumugwe: Hackberry

L

Lakshmi: Deodar cedar, privet
Liber: Plum
Loki: Eastern red cedar, elm, willow, yew

M

Mars: Cherry, hawthorn
Mary: Wisteria
Mercury: Pecan
Minerva: Ash, olive
Momotaro: Peach
The Morrigan: Black locust, eastern red cedar, cherry, oak, willow

N

Nott: Datura
Nut: Sycamore
Nyambe: Padauk
Nyx: Datura

O

Obatala: Ebony
Odin: Ash, beech, elm, yew
Osiris: Deodar cedar, Douglas fir, sycamore

P

Paean: Tulip tree
Pan: Douglas fir, pine
Parvati: Privet
Picumnus: Plum
Pluto: Poison ivy
Pomona: Pear
Poseidon: Spruce, willow
Priapus: Pecan
Prometheus: Wisteria

Q

Qamaits: Sweetgum

R

Ra: Deodar cedar, olive, poison ivy
Rhiannon: Maple
Rudra: Crepe myrtle

S

Saturn: Dogwood, holly, mimosa
Sekhmet: Witch hazel
Selene: Datura
Serket: Witch hazel
Shiva: Deodar cedar
Sita: Deodar cedar
Sucellus: Hornbeam

T

Ta-Bitjet: Witch hazel
Thoth: Poison ivy
Thor: Birch, black walnut, cherry, hawthorn, oak, rowan
Tyr: Eastern red cedar, cottonwood, holly, poplar

V

Venus: Elder, maple, orange, peach, pear, pine, plum
Vishnu: Black walnut, privet
Vulcan: Elder, rosemary, rowan

Y

Yamaya: Ebony

W

Wah'kon-tah: Osage orange
Winalagalis: Sweetgum
Wong Tai Sin: Ginkgo, witch hazel

Z

Zeus: Apple, beech, black walnut, chestnut, hawthorn, oak, olive, willow

Appendix B
Woods by Uses

Wood	Uses
Alder	Protection, water rituals
Apple	Love, deception
Ash	Prosperity, weather magic
Beech	Health, exorcism of pests
Birch (river or white)	Water rituals, winter solstice
Black locust	Strength, binding another's will to you
Black walnut	Dark protection, protection against sickness
Cedar, deodar	Meditation, healing
Cedar, eastern red	Money magic, business magic
Cherry	Love, immortality
Chestnut	Divination, spiritual cleaning
Cottonwood	Annoyance, dark energy
Crepe myrtle	Escape, politics
Datura	Cleansing of negativity

Wood	Uses
Dogwood	Ancestral magic, Southern root magic
Douglas fir	Wilderness magic, safety
Ebony	New moon magic, defense
Elder	Fairy magic, protection of your soul
Elm	Chaos magic, dealing with the dead
Fig	Deception, eliminating shame or guilt
Ginkgo	Longevity, defense against aging
Golden rain tree	Exploration, travel
Hackberry	Cleaning, menstruation
Hawthorn	Dying, working with the Fae
Hemlock	Building, cleaning
Hickory (shagbark)	Healing, death rituals
Holly	Positive magic
Hornbeam	Strength, gardening
Laurel	Divination, creativity
Magnolia	Southern heritage magic, connecting with Gaia
Maple	Love, flight in thought and deeds
Mimosa	Dance magic, offensive magic of throat and lungs
Mulberry	Courtship magic, love
Oak	Protection, strength

Wood	Uses
Olive	Avoiding issues, purity
Orange	Prosperity, love
Osage orange	Keeping things either in or out, ancestral magic
Padauk (African variety)	Dark energy, annoyances
Peach	Love, exorcising baggage
Pear	Love, sexual arousal
Pecan	Money, employment
Persimmon	Water protection, gender fluidity
Pine	Fertility, longevity
Plum (purple leaf)	Cooking magic, cleaning
Poison ivy	Dark magic
Poplar	Fairy work, entry to the underworld
Privet	Separation
Rosemary	Lightning magic, protection from lightning
Rowan	Fertility, connecting to the gods
Spruce	Flight magic, building
Sumac	Earth connection
Supplejack	Dark enenrgy, defense
Sweetgum	Energy magic, healing nerves
Sycamore	Fire magic, divination

Wood	Uses
Tulip tree	Healing, working with the underworld
Willow	Healing, health
Wisteria	Clarity, illumination for learning
Witch hazel	Healing, cleaning residual energies
Yew	Dream weaving, protection

Bibliography

Ananda, Galaihalage K. S., Harry Myrans, Sally L. Norton, Roslyn Gleadow, Agnelo Furtado, and Robert J. Henry. "Wild Sorghum as a Promising Resource for Crop Improvement." *Frontiers in Plant Science* 11 (2020). https://doi.org/10.3389/fpls.2020.01108.

Andrews, Alfred C. "Acclimatization of Citrus Fruits in the Mediterranean Region." *Agricultural History* 35, no. 1 (1961): 35–46. https://www.jstor.org/stable/3740992.

Baker, Charlotte. "Brooms and Besoms: History and Lore." *Enchanted Living Magazine* (blog), October 30, 2019. https://enchantedlivingmagazine.com/brooms-and-besoms-history-and-lore/.

Berenji, Janoš, Jeff Dahlberg, Vladimir Sikora, and Dragana Latkovi. "Origin, History, Morphology, Production, Improvement, and Utilization of Broomcorn [Sorghum bicolor (L.) Moench] in Serbia." *Economic Botany* 65, (2011): 190–208. https://doi.org/10.1007/s12231-011-9155-2.

"Besom." Merriam-Webster. Accessed September 5, 2024. https://www.merriam-webster.com/dictionary/besom.

"Broom." Brooklyn Museum. Accessed September 30, 2023. https://www.brooklynmuseum.org/opencollection/objects/118434.

"Brooms/Brushes of Vegetable Material." The Observatory of Economic Complexity. Accessed February 6, 2024. https://oec.world/en/profile/hs/broomsbrushes-of-vegetable-material?redirect=true.

Carter, P. R., D. R. Hicks, A. R. Kaminski, J. D. Doll, K. A. Kelling, and G. L. Worf. "Broomcorn." Accessed 9/30/2023. https://hort.purdue.edu/newcrop/afcm/broomcorn.html.

Chaucer, Geoffrey. *The Canterbury Tales*. Translated and edited by Nevill Coghill. Penguin Classics. Penguin Books, 2003.

Cherry, Ron, and Hardev Sandhu, "Insects in the Religions of India." *American Entomologist* 59, no. 4 (2013): 200–202. https://www.researchgate.net/figure/Jain-monks-wear-mesh-over-their-faces-to-avoid-inhaling-insects-and-carry-soft-brooms-to_fig1_262855310.

"Chestnut-tree." McClintock and Strong Biblical Cyclopedia. Accessed February 11, 2025. https://www.biblicalcyclopedia.com/C/chestnut-tree.html.

Dirr, Michael. *Manual of Woody Landscape Plants: Their Identification, Ornamental Characteristics, Culture, Propagation and Uses*. 6th ed. Stipes Publishing, 2009.

Dundes, Alan. "'Jumping the Broom': On the Origin and Meaning of an African American Wedding Custom." *The Journal of American Folklore* 109, no. 433 (1996): 324–29. https://doi.org/10.2307/541535.

Editors of the *American Agriculturist*. *Broom-Corn and Brooms: A Treatise on Raising Broom-Corn and Making Brooms on a Small or Large Scale*. New and revised ed. Orange Judd Company, 1908.

Fee, Christopher R., and Jeffrey B. Webb, editors. "Jumping the Broom." In *American Myths, Legends and Tall Tales: An Encyclopedia of American Folklore*. Vol. 2: G–P. ABC-CLIO, 2016.

"From Benjamin Franklin to Jane Mecom, 21 February 1757," Founders Online. National Archives. Accessed September 30, 2023. http://founders.archives.gov/documents/Franklin/01-07-02-0048.

Harper, Clive. "The Witches' Flying-Ointment." *Folklore* 88, no. 1 (1977): 105–106. https://doi.org/10.1080/0015587X.1977.9716057.

Hobbs, Karen. *Swept Away: The Vanishing Art of Broom Making*. Schiffer Publishing, 2017.

Huber, Hugo. "Adangme Purification and Pacification Rituals (West Africa)." *Anthropos* 53, no. 1/2 (1958): 161–91. http://www.jstor.org/stable/40453193.

Jones, Daniel. "Broom Corn and Brooms: The History of Broom Corn Cultivation and Broom Manufacturing in Iowa." Theses and Dissertations.

Iowa State Digital Repository, 2005. https://doi.org/10.31274/rtd-20200616-16.

"'Jumping the Broom,' a Story Not a 'Leap of Faith.'" African American Registry. Accessed February 6, 2023. https://aaregistry.org/story/jumping-the-broom-a-short-history/.

Longfellow, Henry Wadsworth. "The Village Blacksmith," Poets.org, accessed December2, 2024, https://poets.org/poem/village-blacksmith.

Lowder, J. Bryan. "How the Broom Became Flat," Slate, June 6, 2012, https://slate.com/human-interest/2012/06/broom-history-how-it-became-flat.html.

Minney, Nicola. "Superstitious in the Countryside: Ten British Farming Superstitions." *The MERL* (blog), October 31, 2020. https://merl.reading.ac.uk/blog/2020/10/superstitious-countryside/.

Mooney, James. "The First Fire." In *Myths of the Cherokee*. Extract from the Nineteenth Annual Report of the Bureau of American Ethnology. Government Printing Office, 1902. https://www.gutenberg.org/files/45634/45634-h/45634-h.htm.

Morgan, Kate. "The Sweeping Appeal of Handcrafted Brooms." *Washington Post*. November 3, 2023. https://www.washingtonpost.com/home/2023/11/03/craft-brooms-enjoy-increased-popularity/.

Muenzler, Georgia. Lecture, master's program of landscape architecture. University of Oklahoma, 1989.

National Garden Association. "Harvesting Broom Corn—Knowledgebase Question." Accessed October 1, 2023. https://garden.org/frogs/view/14292/.

Nedelcheva, Anely M., Yunus Dogan, and Paolo Maria Guarrera. "Plants Traditionally Used to Make Brooms in Several European Countries." *Journal of Ethnobiology and Ethnomedicine* 3, no. 20 (2007): https://doi.org/10.1186/1746-4269-3-20.

Olney, Warren. "History of Early American Brooms and Broom Making." BroomShop.com. Accessed September 30, 2023. http://broomshop.com/history/.

Parry, Tyler. "Jumping the Broom and the American Cultural Divide." Black Perspectives. African American Intellectual History Society. February 7, 2018. https://www.aaihs.org/jumping-the-broom-and-the-american-cultural-divide/.

Pruitt, Sarah. "Why Do Witches Ride Brooms? The History Behind the Legend." History. Updated August 9, 2023. https://www.history.com/news/why-witches-fly-on-brooms.

"Shaker Made: Agriculture & Industry." The Shakers: Americas Quiet Revolutionaries. New York State Museum. Accessed February 13, 2025. https://exhibitions.nysm.nysed.gov/shakers/industry.html

"Shuro Houki: Hemp-Palm Broom." Translated by Tae Yamaguchi. Reviewed Marina Izumi. Japanese Traditional Crafts. Japanese Traditional Culture Promotion & Development Organization. Accessed September 30, 2023.https://www.jtco.or.jp/en/japanese-crafts/?act=detail&id=300&p=30&c=29.

Skeat, Walter William. "Wipple-Tree, Otherwise Whipultre: Gaytre." In *A Student's Pastime: Being a Select Series of Articles Reprinted from "Notes and Queries,"* Clarendon Press, 1896.

Skelton, Robin. *The Practice of Witchcraft*. Porcépic Books, 1990.

Stojka, Ceija. *The Memoirs of Ceija Stojka, Child Survivor of the Romani Holocaust*. Translated by Lorely E. French. Camden House, 2022.

Thuras, Dylan. "Sex, Drugs, and Broomsticks: The Origins of the Iconic Witch." Atlas Obscura. October 23, 2014. http://www.atlasobscura.com/articles/why-do-witches-ride-brooms.

Tingle, Shari. "Boo Hags Going Bump in the Night." CHStoday. 6AM City Inc. October 26, 2020. https://chstoday.6amcity.com/boo-hags-going-bump-in-the-night.

Wigington, Patti. "Make Your Own Besom." Learn Religions. Updated September 26, 2018. https://www.learnreligions.com/make-your-own-besom-2562738.

To Write to the Authors

If you wish to contact the author or would like more information about this book, please write to the author in care of Llewellyn Worldwide Ltd. and we will forward your request. Both the author and publisher appreciate hearing from you and learning of your enjoyment of this book and how it has helped you. Llewellyn Worldwide Ltd. cannot guarantee that every letter written to the author can be answered, but all will be forwarded. Please write to:

Chelsea Townsnend
Gypsey Elaine Teague
℅ Llewellyn Worldwide
2143 Wooddale Drive
Woodbury, MN 55125-2989

Please enclose a self-addressed stamped envelope for reply, or $1.00 to cover costs. If outside the U.S.A., enclose an international postal reply coupon.

Many of Llewellyn's authors have websites with additional information and resources. For more information, please visit our website at http://www.llewellyn.com.